WOMAN'S RELATIONSHIP WITH HERSELF

Woman's Relationship with Herself explores the relationships that women have with themselves and demonstrates how this relationship is often dominated by debilitating practices of self-surveillance.

Employing Michel Foucault's notion of panoptical power, Helen O'Grady illuminates the link between this kind of self-policing and the broader mechanisms of social control, arguing that these negative practices prevent women from enjoying a satisfying and affirming relationship with themselves. Cultural factors that render women vulnerable to dissatisfying self-relations are identified and analysed and, drawing on the insights of Foucault, feminism and narrative therapy, the possibilities for developing a more empowering relationship with the self are examined.

This innovative contribution to feminist debates about gender and the self will be of interest to students and researchers in social psychology, feminist psychology, mental health studies and gender studies, and to practitioners in psychological therapies and counselling psychology.

Helen O'Grady is currently a Visiting Scholar at the School of Political and International Studies, Flinders University of South Australia. She has also worked as a counsellor in the area of women's health.

D1601524

WOMEN AND PSYCHOLOGY
Series Editor: Jane Ussher
School of Psychology
University of Western Sydney

This series brings together current theory and research on women and psychology. Drawing on scholarship from a number of different areas of psychology, it bridges the gap between abstract research and the reality of women's lives by integrating theory and practice, research and policy.

Each book addresses a 'cutting edge' issue of research, covering such topics as post-natal depression, eating disorders, theories and methodologies.

The series provides accessible and concise accounts of key issues in the study of women and psychology, and clearly demonstrates the centrality of psychology to debates within women's studies or feminism.

The Series Editor would be pleased to discuss proposals for new books in the series.

WOMAN'S RELATIONSHIP WITH HERSELF

Gender, Foucault and therapy

Helen O'Grady

Routledge
Taylor & Francis Group

LONDON AND NEW YORK

First published 2005
by Routledge
27 Church Road, Hove, East Sussex BN3 2FA

Simultaneously published in the USA and Canada
by Routledge
270 Madison Avenue, New York, NY 10016

Routledge is an imprint of the Taylor & Francis Group

Copyright © 2005 Psychology Press

Typeset in Sabon by Garfield Morgan, Rhayader, Powys
Printed and bound in Great Britain by TJ International Ltd, Padstow, Cornwall
Paperback cover design by Anú Design

This publication has been produced with paper manufactured to strict environmental
standards and with pulp derived from sustainable forests.

British Library Cataloguing in Publication Data
A catalogue record for this book is available from the British Library

Library of Congress Cataloging-in-Publication Data
O'Grady, Helen, 1953–
Woman's relationship with herself : gender, Foucault and therapy / Helen O'Grady.
p. cm.
Includes bibliographical references and index.
ISBN 0-415-33126-9 (hard cover) – ISBN 0-415-33127-7 (pbk.)
1. Women—Psychology. 2. Women—Identity. 3. Self-perception in women.
4. Self-esteem in women. 5. Control (Psychology) 6. Sex role—Psychological aspects.
7. Foucault, Michel. I. Title.
HQ1150.O47 2005
155.3'33—dc22
2004014321

ISBN   0-415-33126-9 (hbk)
ISBN   0-415-33127-7 (pbk)

For Kerri and James

CONTENTS

ACKNOWLEDGEMENTS

I am indebted to the American Association of University Women without whose funding I would have been unable to produce this book. I also greatly appreciated the working environment provided by the Centre for Interdisciplinary Gender Studies at the University of Leeds and in particular the support and encouragement of its director Sasha Roseneil. Thank you too to my wonderful colleagues in Adelaide's women's health centres and to all the women whose stories of pain, hardship, achievements and triumphs inspired this work. Finally, heartfelt thanks to Margaret Wild for her unfailing faith in my ability to complete this project.

The ideas in this book were first outlined in an essay called An ethics of the self, in Dianna Taylor and Karen Vintges (eds), *Feminism and the Final Foucault*. Urbana & Chicago: University of Illinois Press, 2004.

INTRODUCTION

This book is about women's relationship with themselves. It is about the quality of this relationship, whether it tends to be kind, loving, harsh, guilt-ridden, accepting, appreciative, ashamed, trusting, punitive, hateful, compassionate or perhaps a mix of these or other qualities. It is about the different types of social forces influencing women's attitudes towards the self. The relationship women have with themselves is not something we hear much about. More common is talk about women's relationships with others – with children, men, parents, siblings, other women, and so forth. This is not surprising as historically feminine identity largely has been defined, and thus often experienced, in terms of connections with others. This highlights one reason why a focus on the relationship women have with themselves is important. Foregrounding this relationship is one way of refusing to accept an historically defined identity over which women have had little say. Moreover, dominant western definitions of what it means to be a woman have been biased heavily towards male ideas, desires and prejudices and, as such, are likely to be problematic for women. For example, historically women have not been defined as beings in their own right but in terms of how they stand in relation to men – for example as emotional rather than rational, as physically weaker, as domestically rather than publicly oriented, and so on. In this process women have been designated "the second sex", that is, secondary to men. While not wanting to downplay the significance of feminist achievements, the legacy of sub-ordinate status continues to influence women's lives in various institutional, social and psychological ways. Furthermore, the common emphasis on women's caretaking responsibilities has tended to discourage any roughly equal focus on care for women's selves. Indeed caring for others often has been *at the expense of* women's own needs, desires and goals. In light of both the legacy of cultural inferiorization and an imbalance between caring for others and caring for oneself, women's self-relationship can be seen as a casualty of traditionally defined female identity.

Speaking in very general terms, what might characterize the type of relationship with the self that emerges from many western women's

1

cultural experience? Unsurprisingly, the lack of value and affirmation associated with the legacy of secondary status is likely to generate varying levels of self-doubt or a diminished sense of worth. For many women this may be compounded by the self-renunciation implicit in their socially designated role as the caretakers of others. An imbalance between caring for others and caring for the self tends to generate a need to please and accommodate others. Dependence on the approval of others can render one vulnerable to feeling never quite good enough. These (and other) factors can contribute to women experiencing uneasy or conflictual relationships with themselves that often are characterized by feelings of inadequacy, guilt, shame or dislike. While the degree or intensity of such feelings is likely to vary both for individuals (according to personal experience) and among different groups of women (according to positions of privilege or disadvantage in terms of social relations of race, class, sexuality, health, etc.), anecdotally the notion of uneasy self-relations resonates for women from a diverse range of backgrounds and experience. This suggests that even those in relatively advantageous positions are not immune to social processes which devalue and discount women's experience. In this light, the issue of a woman's self-relationship can be examined as an effect, albeit variable, of gender oppression.

This book attempts to make more visible some common practices which reflect dissatisfying or debilitating ways of relating to the self and to explore possibilities for transforming these. Often negative ways of relating to ourselves have become so automatic and seemingly second nature that it is hard to recognize their existence as separate from who we are. In this way, disabling self-relations tend to be experienced as an inevitable part of identity rather than something we can have a say about or gain some control over. The purpose of foregrounding woman's self-relationship is precisely to challenge this assumption. Once the culturally constructed nature of this relationship becomes evident so too does the potential for fashioning it more in line with our own choices and preferences. For some women this may involve developing more accepting, kind, humorous, loving or playful ways of relating to themselves – orientations so often reflected in relationships with others. Moreover, once women start to participate more actively in shaping their self-relationship, greater freedom of choice about broader questions of identity begins to emerge – for example about what it means to be a woman, a mother, an intimate partner, a sexual being, a daughter, a friend, a professional, and so on. This is because the compelling need to conform to other people's/society's expectations diminishes with increased self-regard. This type of orientation towards the self generates the confidence required to question and move beyond self-understandings experienced as unsatisfactory. This is not to suggest that developing a different type of relationship with oneself is likely to occur overnight. Given the habituated nature of existing self-relations and the various ways, subtle or otherwise, that negative attitudes towards women's selves continue to be affirmed in the broader culture, this is unsurprising. Movement towards a revised self-relationship is likely to be an ongoing, dynamic process. This type of project calls on different levels of self-knowledge. Most importantly it is a journey of the heart. As we become increasingly open-hearted towards ourselves, the prospect of enjoying a different type of self-relationship increases as do more enabling self-understandings. In this process, we become better able to negotiate a roughly equal place for our own needs and desires alongside those of others. Over time a richer description and experience of the self becomes available.

The development of identity practices more in line with different women's voices does not imply a shift beyond the social realm to some purely individualized space. The idea that underneath all psychological, social or historical determinants there lies a true, untainted self is a common assumption in western culture. Yet such a notion belies the significant role played by history and culture in shaping different notions of selfhood at specific moments within and across cultures. It also ignores the way in which selves are constituted along multiple lines in relation to social categories of race, class, sexuality, health, and so forth. When sociohistorical factors are taken into account, the idea of an intrinsic or essential self can be seen as one cultural construction among others. In this light, the move towards greater self-authorship involves having more of a say about which culturally available ideas and practices best reflect our preferred values and beliefs. This can include ways of thinking and living which challenge commonly accepted norms and standards. This type of self-making requires creative interaction with given identity practices as we begin to choreograph our own steps in a dance with the various forces that seek to shape us. Moreover, precisely because of the culturally constructed nature of self-making this is an ongoing, open-ended activity.

LOCATING THE AUTHOR

When authors are transparent about the motivation informing their interest in a topic, the reader is offered an explanation of why that particular subject is a focus of concern. This can provide a useful reference point in efforts to make sense of and evaluate the work. This type of transparency also helps avoid any assumption of author neutrality. Such an assumption obscures the reality that all positions, frameworks or views offer a particular perspective, including ones that claim or assume impartiality. My own interest in the type of practices characterizing women's self-relationship derives from working in the Women's Health sector in South Australia. In a counselling context, I began hearing women talk about having to live with something one woman named as an ongoing "internal battle". In trying to better understand this phenomenon, which clearly was not restricted to women seeking counselling, I have found the work of philosopher and historian Michel Foucault helpful. Hearing about the pain of these inner battles that frequently accompany women through the course of their everyday lives (lives that for some women also involve various external struggles of violence, abuse, discrimination, poverty, legal injustice, loss, etc.) breathed life into Foucault's claim that policing one's own thoughts, feelings and actions to ensure conformity to commonly accepted ideas and practices is an ingrained mechanism of social control in modern western societies. This effectively means individuals living their lives as though under constant observation. Exploring this notion in relation to women's lives seemed a way of getting at something whose internal location and introspective nature tend to render it outwardly invisible, to the extent that women can appear to be coping reasonably well yet nonetheless be engaged in punitive and exhausting inner battles. As already mentioned, these battles tend to be experienced as an inevitable or automatic part of identity. As such they often have women feeling as though they are personally deficient. In Foucault's terms, this can be seen as a great success in relation to social control as it has individuals taking responsibility for problems and struggles regardless of the social context in which these are occurring. In Chapter 2, I discuss some common self-policing practices in women's lives. Self-policing is the umbrella term I use to describe a range of debilitating internal practices. An exploration of such practices sheds light on some of the interrelated psychic and cultural processes which undermine women's self-belief and confidence. Exposure of the relationship between individual struggle and socially privileged ideas, practices and structures reflects the link between experiences of selfhood and the broader power structures of society.

The broad resonance of notions of self-policing among diverse groups of women both within and beyond the counselling context suggests that self-policing practices are not confined to any one group of women – for example women who seek therapeutic services or, more specifically, women whose sense of self has been shattered, or poorly formed, by the trauma of abuse. This is not to imply a uniformity of experience as, clearly, once factors other than gender are considered, a multiplicity of intersecting influences are likely to affect the frequency and intensity of self-policing activity. Nonetheless, identifying effects of gender oppression continues to be an important part of social justice struggles and provides a basis for examining differences among diverse groups of women. In addition, illuminating commonality has the potential to lessen the distress, sometimes despair, experienced by certain groups of women about the perceived gap between them and so-called "normal" women. One example may be women who have been subjected to childhood sexual abuse. For some survivors of abuse, this perceived difference at times can be experienced as a painful yearning to bridge a gap constantly felt to be out of reach. In this context, it is frequently a surprise and relief to learn that women who have not been subject to abuse also often struggle with voices of self-doubt, self-criticism and self-blame. As long as this information is conveyed in a way that clearly does not trivialize or minimize the frequently more intensified experience of those who have been subjected to the trauma of abuse, it can soften an often absolute sense of "otherness" felt by some survivors. When this occurs, the power of one of the most desolate legacies of abuse is disturbed. Moreover, acknowledging the common existence of self-policing among women has the potential to work back the other way. It can help bridge the divide often assumed on the part of women who have not been subject to violence or abuse. This has the potential to encourage a greater sense of connection and empathy by the latter group as well as increased understanding, compassion and, importantly, admiration for those struggling with the debilitating effects of more heightened self-policing.

Nonetheless, it is important to stress that reference to the common nature of self-policing should not be construed as conflating differences among women. Cultural invitations to self-police in line with dominant identity norms clearly are likely to exert less of a hold for women who simultaneously occupy sites of social privilege, for example in relation to class, race, sexuality or health. For women in these categories, the impact of gender enlarged self-doubt is likely to be moderated (though frequently not eliminated) by the sense of entitlement commonly afforded by a middle-class upbringing, whiteness, heterosexuality or good health. Some women may be socially advantaged in some respects – for example in relation to skin colour or sexuality – and disadvantaged in others – for instance in relation to class or health, and so on. This discussion of self-policing aspires towards some kind of (precarious) balance between commonality and difference which invites a much fuller exploration of self-policing experiences among diverse groups of women.

Finally, the particular approach underpinning this book is motivated by a desire to counter the common belief that failure to conform to various social standards and norms is a result of personal deficiency. Such a belief obscures the power of influential ideas or bodies of knowledge to define who we are (for example, heterosexual, white, able-bodied/minded, mothers, self-contained, slim, successful in certain ways, and so forth). Moreover the belief in personal deficiency, so frequently (though by no means exclusively) held by women who seek counselling, is crucial to the power of self-policing. If such a belief is replicated in the therapeutic (or any other) environment this type of internalized oppression is likely to be reinforced. Conversely, exploring the social context of women's ways of relating to and understanding the self allows consideration of the personal impact of influential ideas and practices and enables freedom from often immobilizing feelings of self-blame. It also generates a sense of what different women have been up against in their struggles in life and increases possibilities for an appreciation of their achievements in the face of this. This type of knowledge enhances the potential for desired change. It, moreover, points to the political nature of work on the self which seeks to transform oppressive identity practices (this point is elaborated in Chapter 6).

SOME PRELIMINARY COMMENTS

Before providing a brief overview of the following chapters, several preliminary comments may put to rest, or at least address, certain concerns or questions. First, the type of self-policing practices referred to throughout the book are those which give rise to harsh and debilitating relations with the self and which tie women to unwanted or unsatisfactory self-understandings. Clearly there are many self-policing practices which do not fall into the first category and are of little concern, in terms of their effects, in relation to a person's sense of identity. These might include taking reasonable care of one's health to ensure quality of life or behaving in ways that enable one to live in relative harmony with others; there are also useful habituated disciplines such as washing clothes, replenishing food supplies and generally following established procedures for a whole range of mundane activities. The usefulness of this type of self-policing is highlighted by bringing to mind the difficulties involved in negotiating daily life in a new culture. On arrival, much of what needs to be done has to be thought about and investigated and then gradually, through habituation to the norms of the culture, this knowledge forms part of the background understandings which require little conscious attention.[1] This is not to imply the impunity of various daily routines from critical scrutiny but rather that a certain amount of adherence to routine procedures is a necessary framework for living and is not necessarily oppressive. Furthermore, in discussing self-policing I am not referring to the type of reflective critique to which one might periodically subject one's values, attitudes, desires or actions in order to consider their impact and the desirability or necessity for change. This type of reflection is both healthy and ethically important. By contrast, I am talking about debilitating, often immobilizing, types of self-surveillance and self-castigation which give rise to feelings of personal inadequacy or failure and tend to close down options for change.

Second, as is quite evident, this book focuses exclusively on self-policing practices in relation to women. This is not, however, to imply the absence of such practices in men's lives. Even in the case of socially privileged (white, middle-class, heterosexual, mentally and physically able) males, expectations to conform to inflexible ideas about masculinity can close off a range of other, more desirable ways of being. For instance, what might be the cost to men of policing themselves against any acknowledgement or expression of a feminine side? There also is the problematic, sometimes fatal, issue of men failing to take care of their health because of a conflict between this type of self-attention and certain norms of masculinity. The issues of male on male violence and high rates of male youth suicide are further examples. Thus, although there are enormous advantages to occupying a privileged male position, traditionally defined masculinity also exacts costs. At the same time, oppressive practices of the self are likely to impact more adversely on men who are socially disadvantaged in terms of race, class, sexuality, and so forth. Nonetheless, as Christopher McLean points out, to acknowledge costs associated with dominant forms of masculinity is not to support a position which places male suffering and female oppression on an equal footing. The gendered nature of socialization processes ensures that males and females internalize different *and unequal* self-understandings. Moreover, dominant male identity practices are implicated in female subordination. In McLean's view, men themselves need to develop a more sophisticated understanding of male experience, one that does not avoid the reality of gender inequality and associated domination and exploitation. Such an understanding would both acknowledge the reality of men's suffering as a consequence of conforming to dominant notions of masculinity and simultaneously recognize that these play a part in perpetuating structures that oppress others (McLean, 1996, pp. 11, 24–25). Acknowledging this important difference, however, does not preclude the possibility of some overlap between the sexes in relation to self-policing. This may be the case for women and men who occupy socially disadvantaged race, class, sexuality and health positions.

The third point of qualification relates to the focus on internal psychic processes. Concentrating on this aspect of experience is motivated by the view that the relationship women have with themselves is one level at which the struggle to move beyond an imposed sense of identity takes place. Nonetheless, this does not imply that other levels of women's struggle for greater self-definition are less important. Indeed given the relationship between cultural ideas, structures and practices and the process of identity formation, broader social change is crucial. Even in the face of such change, however, psychic struggles may continue. Moreover, the relative invisibility of such struggles means they are less likely to find a voice. As noted, self-policing tends to be experienced as an automatic part of thinking and thus as reality. This makes it a particularly insidious form of oppression. Its ability to encourage individuals to ignore the social context of their experience and convince them of personal inadequacy can be even more undermining in a cultural environment which has become less exclusionary for women. If it is now possible for more women to move into previously prohibited areas of social life, internal barriers to fulfilment or achievement easily can translate into a sense of personal failure, engendering feelings of hopelessness or disempowerment. In this light, an investigation of self-policing can be seen to highlight one aspect of women's struggle for greater self-definition and to complement equally important struggles at the broader level of social structures, institutions and processes.

Fourth, while this book aims to illuminate the often obscured power of influential ideas and practices to define personal identity and experience, it is not intended to depict women as passive victims of patriarchal power. Evidence of resistance to the dictates of self-policing and associated identity prescriptions always is present. Moreover, as indicated, the purpose of highlighting self-policing is to facilitate its transformation or at the very least to reduce its harmful effects. This calls on women's active participation in negotiating given power relations in efforts to forge identity practices over which they have a greater say. Finally, this book primarily discusses self-policing in a therapeutic context. Nonetheless, this is not the only environment in which this issue can be thought about or challenged. Moreover, although I advocate a particular therapeutic approach, it is not meant to imply that all its aspects are unique. While taken as a whole this approach offers a distinctive orientation, certain practices will reflect an overlap with other therapies.

LAYOUT

The themes introduced above unfold throughout subsequent chapters. While each chapter focuses on specific aspects in relation to self-policing, the overall concern is to explore ways in which the negative effects of such a practice might be healed through a retelling of oneself. This exploration draws on Foucauldian and feminist insights and the ideas and practices of narrative therapy and relational externalizing. Chapter 1 elaborates Foucault's idea of panoptical power as a useful framework for understanding practices of self-policing. It then locates this analysis in his broader critique of western modernity which expands the discussion of modern identity practices and provokes reflection on how we might begin to think and act beyond our current limits. Central to Foucault's critique is a challenge to conventional assumptions about the existence of an underlying human core or essence. Discussion centres on the way in which such a notion both constrains human creative capacities for self-fashioning and generates social practices of exclusion. While the challenge to essentialism threatens to disturb deeply cherished cultural convictions, at the same time it importantly opens space for developing an ethos of critique and transformation of self-understandings that have taken on the appearance of the natural. For Foucault, actively engaging in such an ethos represents freedom. Rather than being some kind of final state wrested from power's influence, however, freedom is redefined in terms of ongoing negotiation with existing power relations. I argue that this critique of modern identity practices and the transformative possibilities it suggests offer a significant contribution to contemporary discussions of self-policing.

Having claimed Foucault's thought as a useful explanatory framework, his failure to consider the impact of gender on self-policing nonetheless is deemed problematic. The fundamental role of gender in identity-forming processes makes it a crucial variable in any examination of internal practices alleged to reinforce the status quo. In Chapter 2, I point to two cultural factors – the historical legacy of secondary status and a common imbalance between care for others and care for the self – likely to heighten women's vulnerability to self-policing and associated identity prescriptions; this discussion touches on aspects of a debate among feminists about the wisdom of developing a morality characterized by an ethics of care for others. I then go on to examine some self-policing practices which commonly structure (aspects of) women's self-relations. These include self-surveillance, ongoing self-judgement, a debilitating type of self-criticism, unfavourable comparisons with others and personal isolation or alienation. This is followed by discussion about the difference in identity processes for diverse groups of women. It is claimed that the intensity of self-policing is likely to vary according to women's position in relation to social divisions of race, class, sexuality, health, and so forth, and experiences of violence and abuse.

Chapter 3 looks at a therapeutic approach, commonly known as narrative therapy, whose ethical and political framework is compatible with a feminist analysis of self-policing. This is reflected in its concern about the way in which therapy may be reproducing broader cultural "truths" and inequities that contribute to the very problems people are seeking to address. This gives rise to a critique of key therapeutic assumptions including the notion of individual pathology, essentialism and the idea of the therapist as holder of objective knowledge about people's lives and problems. Key narrative practices include *externalizing*, and *exploring times of difference to*, problematic experience. Externalizing conversations counter the tendency, common in individualistic societies, to perceive problems as a reflection of personal deficiency. As such, they clear space for people to engage actively in revising their relationship with problems rather than being defined by them. This process frequently includes an exploration of the historical, cultural and gender dimensions of problems or concerns. In this way, as well as challenging the power of oppressive internalizing discourses by generating a sense of distance between the person and the problem, externalizing practices explore the influence of social relations of power in generating and/or reinforcing problematic experience. Charting a history of personal resistance indicates the extent to which problems have not got the better of people (often a surprise to them), and provides encouragement for ongoing acts of resistance. In this process, identity practices are renegotiated in line with people's preferred understandings. These emerge from an exploration of their identification with cultural values, qualities and aspirations they prefer over those which historically have shaped their inherited story of identity. Revised identity projects are made more available for performance in daily practices of thinking and living through their validation and reinforcement by sup- portive others. In the final section of the chapter the issue of moral rela- tivism is discussed – that is, whether an approach which eschews the idea of objective truth has any basis for evaluating the relative worth of identity and life narratives.

Chapter 4 presents several strands of critique by practitioners who are sympathetic to key aspects of narrative therapy yet troubled by others. These primarily revolve around the replication of problematic language practices. The most systematic critique of this kind comes from Johnella Bird. Of primary concern is what she sees as the inadvertent reinforcement of a conventional notion of self-regulated identity through an emphasis on the problem as separate from the person in externalization practices. This effectively undermines the commitment to a notion of identity as always formed in relationship to culturally available ideas, practices, time and context. Bird posits an alternative notion of "relational externalizing" as a way of performing, rather than simply valuing, the idea of relational selfhood. I point to the potential of such a notion for destabilizing the idea of self-policing as a fixed aspect of identity.

The challenge to self-policing continues in Chapter 5's discussion of the idea of greater care for the self. Drawing on Foucault's emphasis on the importance of an ethical self-relationship, care for the self is seen to involve an ethos of ongoing critique and transformation of the cultural ideas and practices that shape identity. While this aspect of Foucault's work offers a useful redress to the imbalance in many women's lives between self- and other-care, the Greek-inspired notion of care for the self informing his work on ethics is not without limitations. I point to two feminist accounts which suggest orientations towards the self more likely to facilitate the type of creative self-making championed by Foucault. Specifically advo- cated is the value of friendship as an organizing principle in relations with the self. In the therapeutic context, the practice of relating to the self as one would to a close friend is suggested as an entry point for developing this type of self-relationship. This offers the prospect of women gaining greater access to the levels of care and compassion so often extended to others. Finally, building on a claim by Lois McNay that Foucault's work on ethics exhibits a traditional mind/body split, the chapter concludes with a dis- cussion of some of the detrimental effects of the cultural privileging of rational thought over other ways of knowing when women attempt to embody different identity practices.

Chapter 6 looks at the issue of narrative therapy's use of Foucault's thought in the domain of therapy. At first blush, this might appear paradoxical given Foucault generally is regarded as challenging bodies of knowledge that have constructed categories of illness or pathology. Nonetheless, I argue that this type of therapy reflects the spirit of Foucault's endeavour. An awareness of the link between selfhood and broader structures of power leads to the development of a therapy that aims to assist people to identify and challenge cultural ideas and practices they experience as oppressive. This creates space for the exploration and performance of preferred identity practices. Rather than involving the uncovering of a "true" self, this type of self-making always takes place in relation to culturally available ideas and practices. I argue that in undermining the power of therapeutic discourse to impose an essential identity, narrative therapy subverts dominant identity norms, thereby expanding possibilities for creative, open-ended identity-making. This aligns it more closely with Foucault's project than with the type of therapeutic discourse against which he rails. Discussion of the legitimacy of using Foucault's thought in the therapeutic context is concluded by an examination of two critiques from within the family therapy literature. The final section of the chapter looks at two other important influences in the development of narrative therapy, namely feminism and cultural anthropology, which importantly supplement Foucault's contribution.

The Conclusion draws together the main themes of the book and reflects on the potential for knowledge gained in the therapeutic environment to help counter the negative effects of gendered self-policing in a variety of social contexts.

LANGUAGE PRACTICES

Finally, there are two linguistic points of concern. First, the issue of whether to use first or third person pronouns when talking as a woman about women's experience poses a dilemma. At first sight, the use of third person terms "they" and "their" could imply that I place myself outside the topic of discussion, that I am somehow untouched by practices of self-policing. This is not the case. Indeed the personal resonance of such practices renders them far from purely academic and, in part, has informed my endeavours to fill in some of the intricate detail of their operations. One reason for using the third person, however, is to acknowledge that factors of race, class, sexuality, health, and so forth make what it means to be a woman a very different experience for different groups of women. From this perspective the use of first person pronouns "we" and "our" could be seen to imply inappropriately a homogeneous, uniform group. At the same time, while acknowledging difference among diverse groups of women is crucial, there is nonetheless one advantage to writing in the first person. This is its ability to invoke a sense of inclusion and solidarity in relation to certain common, albeit variable, experiences of sexism. Mindful of the benefits and disadvantages of both approaches, and with some reservations, I have elected to use a mix of both sets of terms with the proviso that the use of "we" and "our" is not intended to imply a uniformity of experience in relation to self-policing.

Second, a brief comment on taken-for-granted language practices. This relates to the common use of dichotomies or binary opposites in much of western thought – for example men/women, reason/emotion, mind/body, subject/object, and so forth. In such binaries the first category gains its distinction through contrast with the second. In recent decades this type of language practice has been criticized strongly by feminists and others for the way it derogates the second part of the binary – women, emotion, body, object, etc. – constituting it as "other". A more generalized example of the entrenched nature of dichotomous thought is the prominence of "either/or" thinking. This type of thought draws a sharp line between supposed opposites, leaving little room for the middle ground where much life experience unfolds, all the more uneasily (perhaps at times not available to awareness) for the absence of language to articulate it. Thus, for example, there is the common expectation to be either for or against people, situations and events, or to see ourselves and others as being either this or that type of person – a coward or hero, confident or timid. Because this type of language practice is so fundamental to our way of thinking it is difficult to avoid. A valuable aid in efforts to move beyond the limitations of binary thinking can be found in Johnella Bird's notion of "language for the in-between". The development of this type of language enables the negotiation of meanings between opposing positions (Bird, 2000, pp. 23–25).[2] Thus rather than talking in terms of absolutes (a confident or timid person, a coward or hero), it becomes possible to speak about *degrees* or *varying types of* confidence or courage or about supporting and/or rejecting *aspects of* divergent positions. This type of linguistic practice allows more of the complexity of lived experience to be acknowledged and articulated. It is my hope that something of the nuance of such an approach has filtered through to this discussion of self-policing. If this is the case, despite the presence of any definitive tenor that may have emerged in efforts to render such a practice more visible and therefore more available for reflection, readers will be able to gain a sense of women's variable relationship to self-policing both in relation to each other and intra-personally. More broadly, it is hoped this discussion may contribute to greater recognition and creative expression of the rich and diverse range of possibilities for selfhood.

1

A LENS FOR VIEWING
SELF-POLICING

> Disciplinary practices . . . secure their hold not through the threat of violence or force, but rather by creating desires, attaching individuals to specific identities, and establishing norms against which individuals and their behaviors and bodies are judged and against which they police themselves.
>
> (Sawicki, 1991, pp. 67–68)

INTRODUCTION

While theoretical explanations are sometimes perceived as onerous (not least when presented in dense, inaccessible forms), at their best they offer interesting, sometimes provocative, ways of thinking about and under-standing a range of human experiences. They provide a space of reflection in which to step back from the immediacy of experience and gain a broader perspective, while at the same time their relevance to concrete practices can be assessed. It is this type of dynamic that I aspire to bring to the discussion of self-policing. One of the key theoretical frameworks informing this discussion is elaborated next. Illuminating the broader cultural context of individual experience, this framework links self-surveillance to the maintenance of contemporary western identities, social standards and norms. This is described by Michel Foucault as a peculiarly modern form of social control replacing earlier more authoritarian mechanisms. Foucault's analysis of self-surveillance forms part of a broader critique which chal-lenges the universalizing tendency of modern thought. Of particular concern is the idea of a human essence or core amenable to the interpretive powers of reason. In his view, such a notion locks individuals into a narrowly defined identity. In seeking to demonstrate the contingent rather than given nature of identity, his historical analyses help disturb over and over again the apparent inevitability of the ways we have come to relate to and understand ourselves. As such, they encourage critique and trans-formation of current practices of self-surveillance and associated cultural

13

norms. Experimentation with different identity practices can draw on Foucault's redefinition of freedom as an ongoing negotiation of existing power relations. Moreover, an emphasis on the sociocultural context guards against the imposition of an "essential" identity.

CONTEXTUALIZING THE PERSONAL

In reflecting on the type of internal struggles frequently described by women – those characterized by varying degrees of self-doubt, self-criticism or self-dislike – Foucault's thought provides a useful framework of understanding. Of particular significance is the link between self-policing practices and the maintenance of dominant identity norms. This type of contextual approach offers an important counterbalance to the individualistic impulse in much of western culture whereby, against clear evidence to the contrary, it often is assumed that who we are and how we live is solely a matter of personal decision or will. Such an assumption places the onus of responsibility for both success and failure largely on individual shoulders. In the case of success this can invite an exaggerated sense of personal achievement, particularly in the socially privileged. In terms of failure, it tends to encourage feelings of self-blame, shame and powerlessness. This is not to deny aspects of identity and life for which we can and should take responsibility but rather that a predominantly individualist orientation obscures the powerful influence of social forces in the construction of a sense of self and life possibilities. Foucault's illumination of the sociopolitical dimension of self-policing helps address this imbalance. From this perspective, while surveillance and judgement of our own feelings, thoughts and conduct in line with generally accepted social standards and norms is an intensely personal experience, it is also part of a broader mechanism which intricately enmeshes the personal and the sociopolitical.

POWER AND KNOWLEDGE

Foucault's notion of self-surveillance as a form of social control is linked to his analysis of the modern system of power. In *Discipline and Punish* (1979) he depicts power as existing in a network of diverse and ever shifting relationships that permeate the entire fabric of society. In his view, conventional analyses which focus on power relations at the level of the state or dominant social groups tend to neglect the small but important everyday workings of power that reach into the depths of society – to the bodies, wills, thoughts, conduct and everyday life of individuals. Power's hold at this "micro-physical" level is such that merely to change a society's

14

economic system or its type of government or institutions would leave untouched a myriad of minute, diffuse and constantly active power relations (Foucault, 1979, pp. 26–27). If such a claim is correct, and the continued presence of women's self-policing in the face of various social advances would seem to support it, this underscores the importance of addressing power relations at the intra-subjective level. Foucault claims that what allows power to exert such a grip is that it is not merely a repressive force but is also creative: "What makes power hold good, what makes it accepted, is simply the fact that it doesn't only weigh on us as a force that says no, but that it traverses and produces things, it induces pleasure, forms knowledge, produces discourse" (Rabinow, 1984, p. 61). In this regard, he points to the pivotal role played by social science discourse in shaping us as beings with certain desires, feelings, habits and dispositions. Thus it is not that particular ways of being are superimposed on who we really are but rather the very stuff of who we are – how we think, feel, behave, our sense of self and what we desire – is fashioned in line with ideas and practices which have come to prominence at a specific historical moment. This linking of systems of power and forms of knowledge contrasts with the conventional view that power acts to repress or deny truth. Such a view is reflected in the widespread belief in an innate or true self constrained by various psychological/social/historical forces of power. For Foucault, however, the very idea of a human essence is itself a product of power. It is an historically specific conception of what it means to be human. To deny this is to foreclose the possibility of freeing ourselves from subjection to an "essential" identity. It blinds us to practices of power which operate through discourses of truth such as those embodied in the human sciences (Owen, 1995, p. 495) – for example the historical construction of sexuality as a defining feature of identity (Foucault, 1978). He therefore rejects the tradition of modern thought in which knowledge can exist and develop only in the absence of power, arguing instead that power and knowledge are mutually constitutive. In this view, no power relation can exist without the constitution of a corresponding sphere of knowledge; nor can knowledge exist which simultaneously does not assume and constitute relations of power:

> truth isn't outside power, or lacking in power . . . truth isn't the reward of free spirits, . . . nor the privilege of those who have succeeded in liberating themselves. Truth is a thing of this world: it is produced only by virtue of multiple forms of constraint. And it induces regular effects of power.
>
> (Rabinow, 1984, pp. 72–73)

Implicit in such a view is a challenge to the conventional understanding of ourselves as "knowing subjects" capable of discerning objective truth. One of the benefits of such a challenge is to undermine the untouchable quality that tends to surround so-called "truth" discourses. This increases prospects for reflection on the ethical implications of the ideas and practices embodied in such discourse. This issue is taken up in Chapter 3's discussion of the therapeutic domain.

THE RISE OF DISCIPLINARY POWER

The idea that we are products, rather than the driving force, of knowledge is reflected in Foucault's history of punishment. Repudiating the conventional view that the practice of incarcerating (rather than torturing or executing) criminals from the end of the eighteenth century reflects a humanitarian advance, he describes instead the emergence of a peculiarly modern form of punishment as discipline. Central to this type of punishment is an attempt to place individuals' everyday lives – their bodily behaviour, identity, activity and seemingly insignificant gestures – under surveillance in order that these undergo correction through the imposition of a rigorous time-table, the development of habits and corporeal constraints. In this light what emerges is "not so much a new respect for the humanity of the condemned . . . as a tendency towards a more finely tuned justice, towards a closer penal mapping of the social body" (Foucault, 1979, p. 78). In this account, disciplinary methods are not confined to institutions such as the prison but gradually permeate broader social relations.

Foucault illustrates his claim about the distinct character of modern power by referring to an ideal architectural form called the Panopticon. Proposed at the end of the eighteenth century by English philosopher and social reformer Jeremy Bentham, its purpose was to enable the constant observation of individual inmates in organizations such as the asylum, hospital, prison, factory or school. Housed in a transparent, circular building featuring a tall central observation tower, inmates are separated from each other and unable to see those observing them. Its principle effect is "to induce in the inmate a state of conscious and permanent visibility that assures the automatic functioning of power" (Foucault, 1979, p. 201). The efficiency and effectiveness of this type of arrangement lie in the fact that both inmates and staff feel under constant pressure to behave in line with the rules of the institution because they can never be certain they are not under surveillance by superiors. In this way they come to scrutinize their own behaviour as the gaze of surveillance turns inwards:

> He who is subjected to a field of visibility, and who knows it, assumes responsibility for the constraints of power; he makes them play spontaneously upon himself; he inscribes in himself the power

relation in which he simultaneously plays both roles; he becomes the principle of his own subjection.

(Foucault, 1979, pp. 202–203)

Although the full implementation of this design never occurs, nor do its many adaptations ever live up to Bentham's intentions (Rabinow, 1984, pp. 19–20), for Foucault this type of panoptical power captures an important dimension of modern reality. In analysing its effects he claims that, while not replacing all other forms of power, it enables power to extend to the smallest and furthest reaches, operating on an anonymous, permanent and mostly silent basis. This involves the constant play of the calculated social gaze which occurs, in principle at least, without an appeal to force, violence or excess.

Foucault contrasts this mechanism of social control with that of the premodern west in which law and order were much more of an authoritarian, top-down affair. While such a system suited the structure of feudal societies, in the late eighteenth century it no longer was an efficient or economical way to govern the developing commercial and industrial states. He depicts the development of disciplinary power as a response to the need to adjust the fit between a significant increase in numbers of people and the growing expansion and complexity of productive forces which call for higher profit levels. It is at this time that the concept of "population" emerges, accompanied by an intense interest in the way a society is governed and the maximization of its resources. According to Foucault, the body and sexuality are central to these concerns. In *Discipline and Punish*, he describes a strategy of meticulous regulation of the bodies, gestures and behaviours of individuals in order to increase their usefulness for institutions such as the military, the hospital, the school and the factory. This new "political anatomy" emerges earlier in some institutional settings than others and in most cases is a response to specific needs, such as industrial progress or a renewed spread of contagious disease (Foucault, 1979). He depicts "bio-power" as the means by which disciplinary methods penetrate all levels of life. This is a form of power which takes charge of the biological processes of the population for the purposes of maximizing its health and well-being, as reflected in an unprecedented concern by governments with specific variables such as rates of birth and death, health, frequency of sickness, fertility, birth control, the character and frequency of sexual activities, legitimate and illegitimate births, the impact of unmarried life, life expectancy, nutrition and housing patterns. In this process, sex assumes strategic importance because of its proximity to the biological processes of both the individual body and the population as a whole. These types of investigations and the policies they generate involve increasingly pervasive "expert" surveillance of the population, and social norms are introduced to ensure regularity in people's behaviour (Foucault, 1978).

17

SELF-POLICING

Foucault claims that while the immediate object of the emerging system of government is to ensure the development of individual welfare in a way that is significant to the state, its ultimate aim is to render its overseer role superfluous by making people agents of their own subjection (Rabinow, 1984, pp. 241–242). This involves individuals incorporating the "gaze" of external authority structures, including dominant cultural ideas and practices, which embody certain prescriptions for thinking and living. Hence the crucial role played by self-policing as a mechanism of social control:

> There is no need for arms, physical violence, material constraints. Just a gaze. An inspecting gaze, a gaze which each individual under its weight will end by interiorising to the point that he is his own overseer, each individual thus exercising this surveillance over, and against, himself.
>
> (Gordon, 1980, p. 155)

The contemporary power of self-policing can be understood, in part, in terms of the pervasive western ethos of individual responsibility and autonomy. The internalizing impulse of such an ethos discourages the contextualization of experience. This is reflected in the widespread belief that, regardless of circumstances, individuals are largely responsible for their own life choices and experience. While taking responsibility for various aspects of one's life is clearly important – for example making the most of available opportunities and feeling as though one has some control over life direction – the overriding individualistic impulse of much of western culture tends to trivialize and obscure the very real effects of social structures which privilege some groups and disadvantage others. A lack of societal acknowledgement of this increases the likelihood of individuals blaming themselves, and being blamed by others, for aspects of life over which they have no control – for example being out of work in communities where largescale economic strategies have resulted in structural unemployment. This type of blame merely compounds the feeling of disempowerment that often accompanies failure to measure up to mainstream standards.

Moreover, self-policing works in the service of what Foucault describes as the modern imperative towards sameness and the pathologizing of difference. This is characteristic of societies in which human worth has come to be measured primarily by the scientific categories of the "normal" and "abnormal" (Foucault, 1979, p. 184). Like the commonly accepted standards and norms it supports, self-surveillance has become such a

18

taken-for-granted part of psychic make up that it is mostly invisible to conscious awareness. This makes it difficult to subject it to reflective scrutiny. Thus, while in one sense it is hard to imagine any torments worse than the physical torture inflicted on the pre-modern French prisoner depicted in the opening page of *Discipline and Punish*, Foucault's portrayal of self-policing importantly highlights the less brutal but nonetheless soul-destroying effects of this modern practice of power. In societies whose basic organizing principle is the group norm, self-surveillance reproduces the constant monitoring, differentiation and ranking of individual conduct "as better than or below average, normal, deviant, and so on" (Allen, 1998, p. 175).

The effectiveness of self-policing seems to lie in its ability to grasp individuals at the very level of self-understanding and the norms governing identity formation (Sawicki, 1998, pp. 94–95). This means that when a person fails to conform to accepted identity modes, aspects, or even the whole, of their sense of self can be experienced as "wrong". For instance, a lesbian or gay person in a society dominated by heterosexism is likely to be acutely aware of the lack of societal affirmation of her or his sexuality, all the more so if she or he is not connected to a supportive gay/lesbian/bi-/transsexual community. Being affirmed culturally is a crucial element of a robust sense of self. The reason its importance often is glossed over, or goes unrecognized, lies in its taken-for-granted pervasiveness in relation to mainstream identities. In the case of heterosexuality, social affirmation is so ingrained in the fabric of everyday existence that it can appear invisible to those being affirmed. To those whose sexuality it silences, however, it is highly visible.

Another example is whiteness. The overwhelming number of ways in which being white is taken for granted and continually affirmed in western cultures renders many white people blind to the fact of having a skin colour at all, let alone to the reality that its social privileging requires the derogation of differently coloured skin. Those constantly subjected to the discriminating "gaze" of white culture are denied the luxury of such colour blindness. Further examples can be seen in relation to gender, class and health. There are also those whose sense of self may have been shattered or poorly formed through the trauma of violence or abuse and whose experience has been silenced by a culture in denial. This is by no means an exhaustive list. Nor, however, is it meant to imply that people cannot or do not protest against marginalization or disadvantage and defy ill-fitting identities and social norms. Resistance is always part of the response to oppression, often in remarkable, and sometimes remarkably successful, forms. At the same time, it is important to remain aware of the myriad ways in which mainstream culture continues to discriminate against those who do not fit its norms and the ceaseless invitations to internalize this oppression.

19

THE BROADER CRITIQUE

Foucault's analysis of self-surveillance forms part of a broader critique which begins with historical analyses of the discourses of madness, clinical medicine and nineteenth-century positivism. These analyses seek to disrupt the conventional wisdom that scientific and rational thought from the seventeenth century onwards represents the unfolding of progressively enlightened knowledge – that is, the belief that in modernity reason increasingly has moved closer to discovering the truth about humanity. Foucault points to the way in which the construction of the human figure implicit in such a view – that of a universal and rational subject of knowledge – has generated practices of exclusion and repression. This is reflected in *Madness and Civilisation*'s account of the classical era's repression of forms of thought not compatible with reason. This results in the constitution of the mad as social "other" and their institutional confinement (Foucault, 1967). Such a process undermines the claim that the integrity of all individuals is respected within Enlightenment rationality (McNay, 1994, p. 27). Moreover, *The Birth of the Clinic* (1973) points to the objectifying effects of practices of scientific classification which gradually permeate the social fabric and play a significant role in mechanisms of social control. This is evidenced in increased "expert" interest in, and regulation of, a broad range of human activities in the modern era. Objectifying practices also tend to be mirrored in individuals' relationships with themselves, their bodies and with others. In relation to the latter, feminists have pointed to the way in which the sexual objectification of women has fostered a sense of male entitlement and proprietorial attitudes in relation to sexual access to females.

Perhaps the single most important idea emerging from Foucault's early analyses is that changes in the way we think do not occur through some type of inevitable historical necessity that reflects unchanging essences. Implicit in the latter view is the notion of some underlying pattern or truth waiting to be discovered by human ingenuity. Foucault disputes this, arguing that social change occurs through human design, error and accident, in other words through concrete human practices which can be altered (O'Farrell, 1989, pp. 38–39). In this light, the idea of an innate subjectivity represents only one possible way of organizing ideas about what it means to be human. While a challenge to essentialism threatens to disturb deeply held convictions, its promise lies in the possibility of greater freedom. For Foucault, the uncritical acceptance of given self-understandings limits and constrains the creative capacity of human beings to intervene meaningfully in identity-formation and to extend the range of possible self-descriptions. Moreover, the idea that reason can provide a true account of human nature is fraught with danger. As alluded to previously, the historical privileging of specific ways of being – white, male, heterosexual, self-contained – has entailed the creation of social "others". This type of cultural inferiorization has concrete effects on people's life choices and possibilities and on a sense of self. In relation to the latter, the disempowering effects of measuring personal worth against given norms and standards also are evident in many women's concerns about body image, looks, weight, personality, happiness, success, and so forth. Foucault's point about the modern imperative for sameness and the pathologizing of difference is pertinent here. Despite the western culture of individualism, simultaneous pressure towards uniformity can make difference from the norm feel anything from mildly to profoundly disturbing. This can result in the imposition of alienating, sometimes dangerous, practices on the body, mind or spirit. The emphasis in Foucault's thought on the historical contingency of the ways we have come to understand ourselves offers a way of undermining "the tyranny of the normal", thereby opening space for a greater appreciation and celebration of our own and others' difference.

POWER-IN-RELATION-TO-FREEDOM

Having focused primarily on the idea of modern identity as an effect of power/knowledge, Foucault subsequently turns his attention to the issue of resistance. He develops the notion of *power-in-relation-to-freedom* which, as James Tully notes, allows him to retain his key insight that humans always act within power relations in the same way that thinking always takes place within structures of knowledge (Tully, 1998, pp. 133, 136–137). Acknowledging the inevitable presence of power in human relationships creates space for thinking about ways in which its effects can be minimized. Thus, while relationships of power clearly can be oppressive, this is not necessarily the case. For example, the teacher–student relationship only becomes so when arbitrary and unnecessary authority is exercised by the teacher (Foucault, 1988, p. 18). Moreover, Foucault claims that when power relations are oppressive resistance is always a possibility. As Jana Sawicki notes, this reflects his view that the social sphere comprises a multiplicity of unstable and diverse relations of power which contain possibilities for both domination and resistance. She gives the example of the knowledge that constructed the homosexual as a certain kind of individual, enabling both the social control of homosexuality by the medical and legal domains *and* a type of resistance in which the identity of homosexual is embraced and demands made for homosexual rights (Sawicki, 1991, pp. 25, 56). In this way given power relations also may provide the means for creative self-expression.

As with the notion of power/knowledge, Foucault's belief in the indissociability of power and resistance contrasts with the dominant western tendency to view power and freedom as mutually exclusive and zero sum. Within such a view increased freedom requires decreased power and vice versa. Conversely, for Foucault freedom must exist for power to be exercised: "Power is exercised only over free subjects, and only insofar as they are free" (Foucault, 1982, p. 221); that is, insofar as they are able to choose from a range of possible ways of acting. In this way, he distinguishes between power relationships which always hold the possibility of reversal and relationships of domination which, because of the extent and immutability of asymmetry between parties, do not. This distinction permits recognition that some social relationships are more entrenched and inflexible than others. Within relations of power, freedom for Foucault is not some kind of final, eternal state wrested from power's influence. Rather it is an ongoing practice of strategic contestation and renegotiation with existing relations of power in which the rules of the game are either modified or challenged (Foucault, 1982, pp. 221–222).

SELF-MAKING PROJECTS

Foucault's later work reflects his interest in the different ways in which individuals can actively constitute themselves as ethical subjects. His genealogy of desire demonstrates that, despite the existence of similar themes and precepts from antiquity through to the present, each historical period is characterized by fundamentally different self-interpretations (Foucault, 1986, 1990). By illuminating this type of historical variability, he seeks to disturb any notion of the inevitability of modern ways of understanding ourselves. The idea that we can become other than we are is particularly important given his view of the restrictive sense of identity provided by psychological and psychoanalytical discourse and corresponding normative disciplines through which he claims we have become victims of our own knowledge of ourselves (Bernauer, 1992, p. 174). In thinking about how to facilitate the development of a different kind of ethics, he advocates a contemporary ethos of self-critique and transformation. This provides a practical means by which to study the limits that constitute us as we are and to experiment with charting a course beyond them. Recent examples of this type of transgression include the "specific transformations that have proved to be possible in the last twenty years . . . that concern our ways of being and thinking, relations to authority, relations between the sexes, the way in which we perceive insanity or illness" (Rabinow, 1984, pp. 46–47). Barry Allen refers to these as

> limited and realistic struggles against . . . the effort to govern people through and because of "who they are" . . . female, homosexual, black, mentally ill, HIV-positive, and so on . . . These

movements assert the individual's right to be different against the power of a scientific and administratively determined identity.

(Allen, 1998, p. 171)

Thus for Foucault, rather than speculating about human nature, critical efforts should be directed towards interrogating and resisting apparently natural and inevitable aspects of identity, including dominant under-standings of rationality, in order to achieve greater freedom of thought. This rules out a conventional view of autonomy as reason free from passion, desires and other empirical factors. In his view, practices of the self through which individuals actively shape their own identities ulti-mately always are determined by the sociohistorical context. His concep-tion of the self, therefore, does not entail any notion of innate potential or a "natural" self (Kritzman, 1988, pp. 50–51). For Foucault, the idea of historically contingent subjectivity offers greater scope for the development and expression of human creative powers.

THE RELEVANCE OF FOUCAULT'S THOUGHT

For the present purposes, the usefulness of Foucault's analysis lies in its demonstration over and over again of the contingency rather than necessity of modern identity practices. This significantly disturbs the taken-for-granted status of the ways we have come to relate to and understand ourselves, thereby increasing possibilities for moving beyond these. As Foucault understood, this is particularly urgent in light of the normalizing impulse of modern culture which has stifled the human creative capacity to fashion a plurality of socially valued identities and ways of life. At the same time, his account of the role played by self-policing in attaching us to given identities helps shed light on the powerful hold of such a mechanism. This enables greater appreciation of the stakes involved in efforts to transform given identity practices which, in turn, can diminish feelings of failure when this proves difficult. It also highlights the significance of past, present and future acts of resistance. Furthermore, once individuals are alerted to the existence of forces beyond personal culpability, the power of self-policing to convince them of the truth of negative self-descriptions is weakened. In this way, a more complex and enabling understanding of the relationship between individual and society than that implied by the idea of self-contained identity begins to emerge.

Just as Foucault's thought allows for the identification of a self-policing mechanism in identity formation, so it also points to the possibility of renegotiating this type of power relation. This is reflected in his advocacy of a practical ethos of critique and transformation of given identity prac-tices. In this process, disempowering ways of relating to and understanding the self can be pinpointed and different possibilities explored. Moreover, while for Foucault this type of self-making constitutes liberty, his redefinition of freedom as an ongoing negotiation of existing power relations offers a realistic description of such projects. Conversely, the conventional view of freedom as some kind of final, power-cleansed state tends to encourage an all or nothing approach. This can have the effect of resurrecting or intensifying the very self-policing practices we want to diminish. It is likely to encourage a view of periodic slippages back to unwanted ways of being as evidence of regression or failure rather than part of the usual process of change. By contrast, the idea of change involving ongoing negotiation with given power relations makes more allowance for the habituated nature of current practices and the continued existence of external constraints. Finally, Foucault's refusal to appeal to any notion of innate identity provides an important safeguard against the imposition of privileged descriptions of the self.

SUMMARY

This chapter pointed to the significance of Foucault's analysis of self-surveillance as a mechanism of social control in modern western societies. Central to this analysis is the depiction of power as a force which both creates, and is reinforced by, systems of knowledge through which modern identity and experience are fashioned. In this account, the individual of modernity has been constituted in line with truths defined by the human sciences and regulated through the internalized "gaze" of authority. Foucault's work on self-surveillance forms part of a broader critique which challenges assumptions about the progressively enlightened nature of modern western thought. This is reflected in his early historical analyses which repudiate the idea of a universal and rational subject of knowledge, arguing instead that human identity and experience are constituted through concrete social practices. It was argued that the relentless emphasis on historical contingency throughout his work helps disturb the taken-for-granted nature of commonly accepted ways of understanding ourselves. For Foucault, the creation of different self-understandings is both possible and desirable in order to enhance the scope for human creativity and generate greater social inclusiveness and diversity. He defines freedom precisely in terms of active participation in the creation of ourselves as other than we are. In his account, freedom is an ongoing practice and one which always takes place within the sociohistorical context.

It is an emphasis on the cultural context of self-policing (and other) practices which renders Foucault's thought useful to a contemporary discussion. This type of contextualization illuminates the link between the structure of individual self-relations and broader mechanisms of power and control. As such, it offers an important counterbalance to exaggerated notions of individual responsibility. This, in turn, encourages belief in the possibility of a different type of self-relationship and the transformation of unwanted identity norms. At the same time, a sociopolitical explanation of self-policing sheds light on the stakes involved in such change. This can increase appreciation of one's past, present and future acts of resistance. Experimentation with different identity practices offers a powerful counter to the "tyranny of the normal" through which individuals are incited towards uniformity and sameness. As such, it has the potential to generate greater diversity and richness in our ways of thinking and living.

Foucault's own work of freedom comes to an end with his death in 1984. While his contribution to modern thought and life continues to be a hotly debated subject, Nancy Fraser has suggested that one of the most important aspects of his legacy is the significant contribution he makes to the politicization of everyday life:

> [Foucault] provides the empirical and conceptual basis for treating such phenomena as sexuality, the family, schools, psychiatry, medicine, social science, and the like as *political* phenomena. This sanctions the treatment of problems in these areas as *political* problems. It thereby widens the arena within which people may collectively confront, understand, and seek to change the character of their lives.
>
> (Fraser, 1989, p. 26)

The politicizing of ordinary life experience reflects one point of convergence between Foucauldian and feminist thought.[1] Having pointed to the relevance of Foucault's thought for a contemporary discussion of self-policing, the following chapter takes up this issue in relation to women's lives.

2

GENDER AND SELF-POLICING

In contemporary patriarchal culture, a panoptical male connoisseur resides within the consciousness of most women: They stand perpetually before his gaze and under his judgment. Woman lives her body as seen by another, by an anonymous patriarchal Other.

(Bartky, 1990, p. 72)

INTRODUCTION

Having portrayed Michel Foucault's thought as a useful framework for understanding self-policing, this chapter seeks to extend his analysis. It considers the impact of gender on self-policing in women's lives. Two factors common to women's experience – the legacy of historical subordination and a frequent imbalance between care for others and care for the self – are singled out as likely contributors to heightened self-policing activity. This is followed by an examination of the type of self-policing practices commonly structuring (aspects of) women's self-relations. These tend to be experienced as a fixed, automatic part of identity and encourage a harsh and punitive relationship with the self. To speak generally about self-policing in women's lives, however, is not to imply a uniformity of experience. While the category of gender can illuminate certain common themes, clearly a multiplicity of factors intersect with gender to render identity processes a different experience for diverse groups of women. It is claimed that the intensity of self-policing is likely to vary according to social location and personal experiences of violence and abuse.

INATTENTION TO GENDER

As outlined in the previous chapter, the limitations and constraints of commonly accepted self-understandings are central to Foucault's concerns.

His analysis of self-policing as an ingrained mechanism for ensuring social conformity provides powerful insight into the maintenance of such understandings in modernity. Yet, while many of the disciplinary practices analysed by Foucault constitute aspects of both female and male identity, he ignores those practices peculiar to female selfhood. This is problematic from a feminist perspective as it takes no account of the cultural inferior-izing of the female body/self (Bartky, 1990, pp. 65, 71). Yet it is precisely this type of difference that renders the relationship between self-policing and gender important. If self-policing ties individuals to given norms and practices, it is likely to play a key role in maintaining aspects of women's subordination. At the same time, factors such as the legacy of subordinate status can enhance the power of self-policing.

THE LEGACY OF SUBORDINATE STATUS

Any exploration of the issue of self-policing in women's lives needs to take account of the cultural inferiorizing of feminine identity. Lois McNay refers to the twin process through which the historical idea that women are inferior to men becomes naturalized through recourse to biology. First, through a comparison with men's bodies and in line with male standards, women's bodies have been posited as inferior. Second, while masculine qualities often can be seen to correlate with dominant conceptions of the male body, for instance strength, aggression, and so forth, man has been conceived of as being able to rise above his biological characteristics through the exercise of rational thought, while woman is portrayed as lacking such a capacity (McNay, 1992, p. 17). While factors other than gender can contribute to an inferior status, in the historical context of subordination it is not surprising that many women find themselves captured by an apologetic mode of being and a general sense of being "less than":

> it is not by chance or as a result of some personal inadequacy that many women find self-doubt an unwanted part of our lives . . . [T]his is understood to be a direct consequence of the ways patriarchy operates in women's lives to undermine our sense of self and thus, through self-surveillance, maintain particular relations of power.
>
> (Swan, 1999, pp. 104–105)

Such a notion corresponds with Jana Sawicki's claim that in various patriarchal contexts a distinctive feature of femininity is "[t]he absence of a sense of self, of one's value and authority, and of the legitimacy of one's needs and feelings" (Sawicki, 1991, p. 106). Sandra Lee Bartky's critique

27

of conventional understandings of shame and guilt sheds light on this type of disempowerment. She claims that within conventional moral psychology, emotions such as shame and guilt tend to be conceived of as playing the important role of reaffirming a person's moral commitments and, in this sense, are "a disruption in an otherwise undisturbed life" (Bartky, 1990, p. 97). In examining the type of shame commonly experienced by women – that which manifests in "a pervasive sense of personal inadequacy" (1990, p. 85) – she argues "there is no such equilibrium to which to return" (1990, p. 97); a person's whole emotional existence may be imbued with a sense of inadequacy. For Bartky, this is understood in light of women's systematic subjection to demeaning treatment in a wide range of arenas in sexist societies. This means that, in addition to more visible structures of disadvantage, shame and guilt can constitute aspects of gender oppression. She claims that such a notion is missing from conventional moral psychology, whose explanation of these emotions lies "almost entirely in its relationship to individual failure and wrongdoing, never in its relationship to oppression" (1990, p. 97). Such an explanation is made possible by positing as universal a privileged male agent "whose social location is such that he has the capacity not only to be judged but to judge, not only to be defined by others but to define them as well" (1990, p. 97). As Bartky notes, such an agent is free from the characteristic types of psychological oppression on which modern class, race and gender hierarchies are so dependent (1990, pp. 90, 96–97).

WOMEN'S HISTORICAL ROLE AS CARERS

Gender subordination is reflected further in women's general training. Central to such training is a "societal assumption that women must define themselves as the caring sex" (Seigfried, 1989, p. 68). In western (and many other) cultures girls are brought up from a very young age to be conscious of, and take responsibility for, the emotional well-being of boys and men. This enables males to take for granted the provision of emotional nurturing. However, such a process is rarely recognized and this lack of acknowledgement allows the idea of male independence and control to be maintained (McLean, 1996, p. 23). The latter is compatible with the sense of self generally associated with masculinity, one distinguished by clear boundaries marking it off from the selves of others. Conversely, the responsibility for emotional nurturance borne by girls and women tends to result in an identity that is more enmeshed in relationship and thus more "other-oriented".[1] This is not to imply the impossibility of some women being generally uncaring towards others or being primarily absorbed with the self. Neither is it the case that men always are oriented more towards the self than others. Rather this is a general claim about the impact of

28

gender socialization processes which tend to ensure, in the case of women, more of an other- rather than self-orientation.[2] While a self- and other-oriented identity need not be mutually incompatible, the emphasis in the training of girls and women on care for others frequently has occurred in the absence of a complementary emphasis on caring for the self (see Jordan *et al.*, 1991, pp. 184–185). Bonnelle Lewis Strickling describes the preparedness to forgo the idea of one's self as a person who merits equal consideration, and a preoccupation with the happiness of others, as characteristic of the ideals traditionally available to women:

> [T]raditionally, women have been asked to be helpful, loving without expectation of return, emotionally dependable, supportive, and generally nurturing to both children and husband both physically and in the sense of nurturing their respective senses of self. . . . [T]aken together, these expectations comprise the expectation of self-renunciation on an extremely large scale.
> (Strickling, 1988, p. 197)

In the earlier discussion of Foucault's work, reference was made to the way in which historically elevated ideas come to assume a natural and inevitable status. The notion of women as emotional nurturers is a prime example. Yet Jean Grimshaw's reminder that this depiction of women was alien to ancient Greek culture (Grimshaw, 1986, p. 63) points to its historical contingency and thus to the possibility of a different construction of caring relations. This is not to imply that caring per se is problematic or something of which we would want less. Rather the self-renunciation entailed in social expectations for women to assume a disproportionate responsibility for the care of others implies a lack of reciprocity in caring relations. In her discussion of historical conceptions of friendship, Peta Bowden refers to the importance attributed to reciprocal relations of care. Drawing on feminist analyses, she notes that the absence of reciprocity, as often is the case between women and men, results in a lack of both external and internal affirmation of self: "[I]n the context of a gendered hierarchy of status and power, women's sense of their own identity, interests and values tends to be both directly disregarded by the structure as well as prone to active self-devaluation" (Bowden, 1997, p. 92). This can give rise to a poorly defined sense of self resulting in the prioritizing of love for others:

> [I]n relations where there is no corresponding affirmation of our own world, as is frequently the case between women and men, we actively assimilate the other's perspective through our concernful and affectionate attention. And perhaps more perniciously, we

may silence or compromise our own values in favour of supplying the requisite emotional support, approval and validation.

(Bowden, 1997, p. 92)

AN ETHICS OF CARE

Despite the centrality of women's nurturing role in society, like all activities undertaken by those assigned an inferior status, it has tended to be devalued. Some feminists have sought to counter this by elevating the more enmeshed, interpersonal mode of selfhood typical of the socialization experience of females.[3] This has given rise to the notion of an "ethics of care" which some feminists have associated exclusively with women. Not all feminists have been comfortable with the revaluation of care for others as a defining feature of womanhood. One concern is about the essentialist implications of such a view. There is also the exclusionary potential of such accounts. For instance, the type of nurture involved in mothering is conceived of by some feminists as central to understanding the more caring ethical standpoint attributed to women. Implicit in such a view is the elevation of mothering above all the other activities women engage in and thus a definition of female identity closely tied to the concept of mother (McNay, 1992, pp. 94–96). What does this imply about the moral worth of women who cannot or do not want to have children? A further concern is that morality characterized by an ethics of care for others may be linked to the occupation of a subordinate status and may, therefore, be characteristic of a range of disadvantaged groups, including men and women from minority groups (Tronto, 1987, pp. 649–652).

Questions also have been raised about the wisdom of automatically assigning a positive value to women's care. Thus Grimshaw argues that, while it is a mistake to depict woman *merely* as victim, it is vital to acknowledge the way in which women are at times disabled and subordinated by the very attributes that also can be their strength (Grimshaw, 1986, p. 202). Continuing this theme Barbara Houston, while recognizing the importance of women's care historically in the nurturance and empowerment of others, is concerned that in the context of unequal economic, political and social relations of power between women and men, an expectation of women's care for others can be used to mask relationships of exploitation and domination in which a woman's own self is sacrificed. In her view, one of the problems with a feminist ethics of care is that if a woman's moral worth is perceived as totally reliant on the ability to care for others, or to be in a relationship, then remaining in harmful relationships may seem acceptable or even necessary (Houston, 1989, pp. 87–89, 93). Similarly, Marcia Homiak argues that when preserving a relationship is seen as more important than its content, emotional support might be provided when other responses may be more appropriate (Homiak, 1993, p. 14).[4] Thus Houston warns of the danger inherent in valuing relations of care outside the context of power relations in which girls and women are devalued and in which there is a considerable level of male violence towards women (Houston, 1989, pp. 91–92). Within such a context little cultural support exists for the type of woman's self required for the practice of a fair and just ethics of care. Such a sense of self would entail:

> a realistic sense of her own competencies and a sense of that which she can reasonably take responsibility for so that she can separate from situations in which caring is not effective and, again, do so without a loss of self.
>
> (Houston, 1989, p. 96)

This corresponds with Joan Tronto's description of moral maturity as entailing a "balance between caring for the self and caring for others" (Tronto, 1987, p. 658).

OVER-RESPONSIBILITY

In the absence of a cultural context encouraging such a balance, the expectation to care for others tends to be internalized as an ethic of responsibility. Grimshaw points to the complex nature of such an ethic. She argues that the emphasis in women's lives on "emotional main-tenance" and preserving relationships has not only engendered a common belief in women that they must maintain relationships, but that they must bear the full responsibility for this (Grimshaw, 1986, pp. 195–196). Because of such a belief

> [t]hey are . . . especially prone to guilt, and to a form of concern for relationships with others which can lead, for example, to the feeling that "not upsetting people" must always be given priority, and that it can *never* be right to do something which will fracture a relationship or break a connection. They are prone, too, to the feeling that they should never put their own needs or desires before those of others.
>
> (Grimshaw, 1986, p. 196)

As indicated, the belief that women are responsible for maintaining relationships can result in a range of disempowering effects (self-denial, exploitation, etc.) Even more pernicious is the way in which such a belief is reinforced negatively through social practices of blame. Joan Laird notes

31

that both mother- and wife-blaming comprise "an important part of almost every major school of developmental and clinical [psychological] theory, including family theory and therapy" (Laird, 1994, pp. 189–190). Indeed over 70 problems for which mothers have been blamed routinely in clinical literature have been documented (Caplan and Hall-McCorquodale, 1985, pp. 345–353).[5] It is only in light of the pervasiveness of mother-blaming ideas that sense can be made of the otherwise baffling frequency with which women are held responsible for the sexual abuse of their children by male family members or friends. One of the most worrying effects of a negative focus on the non-offending parent (most commonly the mother) is to obscure the responsibility of the perpetrator of the abuse (see Freer, 1997).[6] Hence not only does the traditional model of care neglect women's own selves but also can render them culpable for harm inflicted by others. While the sexual abuse of children provides a parti-cularly stark example of misplaced social blame, women also frequently are held responsible when male violence is perpetrated on them. All such blaming practices serve to reinforce the gender-enlarged self-doubt commonly experienced by women.

SELF-POLICING PRACTICES

the rigorous and meticulous self-surveillance, the various self-punishments of the body [mind and spirit] for . . . transgressions, the perpetual self-evaluations and comparisons, the various self-denials, the personal exile, the precise self-documentation.[7]

(White, 1995, p. 45)

It is not hard to see how training in over-responsibility for others, within the historical context of subordination, renders women vulnerable to heightened experiences of self-policing. In such a context there are many incitements for women to monitor rigorously their thoughts, feelings, desires, speech and actions to ensure conformity to accepted rules or the approval of others. This can result in a strict overseer type of relationship with the self, something akin to an overbearing supervisor who continually checks up on workers. This type of self-relationship precludes spontaneity and diminishes possibilities for active participation in the fashioning of one's identity. Moreover, when individuals perceive themselves as having failed to meet accepted norms, this can be experienced not just as a slip up or error but as a transgression against the self – that is, as going to the core of who one is. Such a notion is captured in Bartky's description of the type of shame commonly felt by women:

32

Shame is the distressed apprehension of the self as inadequate or diminished: it requires if not an actual audience before whom my deficiencies are paraded, then an internalized audience with the capacity to judge me, hence internalized standards of judgment. Further, shame requires the recognition that I *am*, in some important sense, as I am seen to be.

(Bartky, 1990, p. 86)

Perceived failure to measure up to accepted standards thus can induce self-punishment. One form this can take is self-castigation. This type of criticism is described by clinical psychologist Marie-Nathalie Beaudoin:

Most women suffer from one type or another of critical voices ranging in intensity. Examples of these are: perfectionism, powerlessness, shyness, anxiety, lack of entitlement (self sacrifice), self-doubt, self-hate, high expectations, comparison, self-blame, and the "if you were a good mother" voice. Other examples even more directly related to our culture are looksism, ageism, sexism, classism, internalized homophobia and racism. These voices can also create and/or support problems such as anorexia, bulimia and depression. In general these voices make women feel like they are never good enough.

(Beaudoin, 1999, p. 1)

This type of criticism usually takes the form of derogatory thoughts about the self (for example: you can't get anything right, you can't be trusted, you're useless, you're a failure, you're so fat, you're unattractive, and so on) which tend to invoke a range of disempowering emotions. These can include feelings of depression, lack of worth, inadequacy, insecurity, hopelessness, anxiety, and so on. Moreover, as Beaudoin further notes, the power of such criticism frequently is reinforced within the broader culture, as for example through media representations of a uniform and unrealistic standard for women's bodies, through the abuse or harassment of girls and women and through an attitude of criticism and perfectionism in the school system (Dickerson, 1998, p. 43). Like all self-policing practices, critical voices tend to be experienced as an automatic, natural part of thinking which makes it difficult to recognize their effects:

It is always incredible to discover how harsh these voices can be and how conditioned and accustomed we are at listening to them and believing them. Most of us would never even consider saying such . . . things to any enemy, yet we accept their daily torture on ourselves.

(Dickerson, 1998, pp. 43–44)

Critical voices frequently co-exist with other punitive practices. Both inside and outside the therapeutic context, women often reveal harsh practices of self-recrimination when judging themselves to have failed to meet certain prescribed norms. Just one example is the imposition of punishing forms of exercise or food deprivation if body weight is perceived to exceed mainstream culture's relentless expectation for slim girls and women. Self-recrimination also can take the form of insidious comparisons with others which inevitably confirm one's worst fears and suspicions. Many of us are familiar with this debilitating practice of measuring ourselves negatively against the perceived qualities or achievements of others. For example, the assumption by a university student grappling with challenging new academic demands that she is less competent than her peers can intensify a sense of inadequacy. This frequently is interpreted in terms of personal deficiency. This type of self-pathologizing can occur in relation to a wide range of everyday activities including parenting, intimate and other relationships, body image and fashion, work, study, and so on. Yet comparing oneself negatively with others leaves little room for an understanding of competency in terms of experience. At times we may be comparing ourselves to others whose skills derive from years of experience. It is also the case that we often overestimate the competencies of others who actually may be struggling with similar feelings to our own. Moreover, pathologizing ourselves tends to bring on amnesia about the times we have been competent. Thus we can feel disconnected from all memory of past and present achievements, or if we do remember these may be stripped of all value so that they no longer feel like achievements.

Seeing oneself as personally deficient also tends to preclude a consideration of cultural factors which may be contributing to feelings of disempowerment. In relation to study, this could include the structuring of academic institutions in what are characteristically male ways of thinking and behaving – for example adversarial styles of debate and competitiveness. Furthermore, for certain groups simply being in a university can generate self-doubt. This may be the case for mature age students who have spent time outside the education system, and whose sense of intellectual ability has been structured, in part at least, by the general devaluing of women. It also may be the case for working-class women stepping into a domain traditionally reserved for the middle class. Many indigenous, black and immigrant women are confronted further by an institution wholly defined and structured by white standards. In a study of American college life, Bartky also refers to the confusing effects of a contradiction between a professed commitment to gender equality at institutional and individual levels and "its actual though covert and unacknowledged absence" (Bartky, 1990, p. 94). She claims that this type of ambiguity, whereby women are in some ways affirmed and in others diminished, tends to create a feeling of inadequacy for many women despite any concrete evidence of failure. Ambiguity also can be a feature of mothering. Despite a general cultural valuing of motherhood, the constraints and pressures of the widespread ethos of mother-blame can have women focused only on the perceived failures of their parenting practices and obscure the social context in which mothering takes place. This can include the lack of affordable, quality child care provision or flexible workplace conditions for the many women who juggle paid work and child rearing, the social stigmatization of single and lesbian mothers and/ or the effects of poverty.

Finally, the possibility of contextualizing one's experience is diminished further by the type of personal isolation that tends to result from negative comparisons with others. By reinforcing a belief in personal deficiency, negative comparisons make a sense of solidarity with others less likely. This type of personal exile reflects the starkest aspect of panoptical power as it involves a belief that: I alone have failed at this particular thing; that there is something wrong with me; that the shame of knowing this puts a barrier between me and others. For Bartky, isolation is characteristic of the secrecy requirements associated with many women's experience of a pervasive sense of inadequacy:

> The need for secrecy and concealment that figures so largely in [this type of] shame experience is disempowering as well, for it isolates the oppressed from one another and in this way works against the emergence of a sense of solidarity.[8]
>
> (Bartky, 1990, p. 97)

Articulating self-policing practices renders their concealed, often taken-for-granted character more visible. This enables an exploration of the impact of such practices on a woman's relationship with herself and others, and an examination of the social context in which they develop and prosper. This type of contextualization plays a crucial role in loosening the stranglehold of a belief in personal deficiency. The knowledge that forces beyond the self have an impact on internal experience and that other women also struggle with voices of self-criticism and self-judgement, helps to free women from immobilizing feelings of self-blame. Once this occurs, the natural or inevitable status of self-policing practices can be challenged. In turn, this opens space for the exploration of alternative, preferred self-relations and increases possibilities for active participation in identity-making. In this light, a focus on women's relationship with the self reveals the potential for renegotiating given relations of power. Chapters 4 and 5 discuss specific ways of achieving this. First, however, I turn to the important issue of differences among (and within) women.

MULTIPLE SITES OF IDENTITY

So far self-policing has been spoken about in general terms. This type of generality is useful for illuminating broad patterns of inequality or oppression deriving from common gender experience. To speak generally of self-policing in women's lives, however, is not to imply a uniformity of experience. To do so would be to ignore the very real differences among diverse groups of women. Mainstream white feminist theory has had to address claims relating to its neglect of the different types of oppression to which women are subject. This debate, led by women of colour in North America in the 1980s, has been important for raising awareness of the way in which gender oppression is mediated by factors of race, class, sexuality, age, able-bodiedness and so on.[9] When factors other than gender are taken into account, it is clear that identity processes vary among different groups of women. Broadly speaking, the experience of being a black or indigenous woman, a working-class woman, or a lesbian is likely to be differently problematic than being white, middle class or heterosexual in cultures which privilege the latter categories and inferiorize the former. As described earlier, this differentiating process entails the creation of an "other" against which privileged categories gain their distinction. With regard to self-policing, if such a practice ensures the measuring of worth in terms of conformity to accepted ways of being, the intensity of the "inner gaze" is likely to vary according to social location and life circumstances. When individuals are positioned beyond "the norm", what constitutes a socially valued identity frequently clashes with experiences of the self – for example, as black, as indigenous, as non-Anglo, as working class, as lesbian/gay/bi- or transsexual, as nonable-bodied, as a single parent, as ill, as fat, and so forth. Moreover, in the case of a constantly visible difference such as skin colour or physical disability, daily exposure to the discriminating gaze of white or able-bodied culture can be unrelenting.

In relation to race, Maria Lugones describes the way that white/Anglo women's behaviour towards women of colour in the USA (neglect, ostracism, stereotyping, labelling as crazy, rendering invisible) results in a lack of recognition; this refusal to see and celebrate the substance of woman of colour robs her of her solidity (Lugones, 1990, pp. 393–394). bell hooks also has written about the impact of internalized racism on African Americans: "Systems of domination, imperialism, colonialism, and racism actively coerce black folks to internalize negative perceptions of blackness, to be self-hating. Many of us succumb to this" (hooks, 1996, p. 32). She notes the importance of the 1960s' black power movement in challenging the psychic effects of white supremacy (hooks, 1996, pp. 119, 121). In the Australian context, Aboriginal magistrate Pat O'Shane points to the ongoing crisis characterizing the lives of many indigenous families and communities as a direct result of colonization. One of the aspects of this legacy has been the internalization of negative characteristics attributed to indigenous people as a standard part of the colonizing process (O'Shane, 1993, pp. 197–198). Some Aboriginal Australians have described the experience of feeling shamed by the gaze of white culture as entailing feelings of embarrassment, disgrace and humiliation (Reclaiming Our Stories, Reclaiming Our Lives, 1995, pp. 27–28).

Yet none of this is meant to imply that members of marginalized or disadvantaged groups cannot or do not develop a critique of dominant culture and construct alternative accounts of identity through a connection to their own knowledges and strengths. The women's movement is a good example of a powerful challenge to dominant norms and practices, as are those emancipation movements initiated by indigenous, black, and gay and lesbian people. Such movements often refuse the dominant culture's definition of their members by celebrating the very qualities it demeans, as reflected in the notion of queer politics or gay or black pride. For instance, hooks identifies self-love as a key strategy of the black liberation struggle of the 1960s (hooks, 1996, p. 119).[10] While not wanting to downplay the significance of such resistance movements in the ongoing struggle for social justice, as noted it is also important not to underestimate the multiplicity of ways in which mainstream culture continues to discriminate against those who do not fit its norms and the ceaseless invitations to internalize this oppression. Thus when factors such as race, class, sexuality, and other broad social categories are taken into account, self-policing is likely to be heightened for members of non-privileged groups. From a feminist perspective, acknowledging multiple sites of identity requires questioning any assumption of gender as the only, or even the primary, site of subordination in a woman's life.

While remaining alert to the multiple sites from which women's identities are constructed, it is also important to bear in mind accounts of sexism from women in marginalized communities. For example, hooks claims that until the silence is broken repeatedly regarding the impact of sexist male domination it will be impossible for African Americans "to constructively address issues of positive gender identity formation, domestic violence, rape, incest, or black male-on-male violence" (hooks, 1996, p. 95). In attempting to maintain awareness of both commonality and difference among women, Susan Bordo's caution against a reaction of immobilization by white feminists to the difference critique may be useful. She argues that while this critique has been crucial in highlighting the need to "struggle continually against racism and ethnocentrism in all its forms . . . nothing [in this critique] . . . declared the theoretical impossibility of discovering common ground among diverse groups of people or insisted that the abstraction of gender coherencies across cultural difference is *bound* to lapse into a pernicious universalisation" (Bordo, 1990, p. 138). hooks appears to agree, arguing consistently that, although an anti-racist agenda must form a central part of an inclusive feminist movement, the existence of white women's racism should not prevent black women and men from participating in feminist politics (hooks, 1996, pp. 100–101, 104).

I have made the general claim that self-policing practices are likely to be intensified for women in socially marginalized groups. Yet at the same time the very experience of marginalization also can render self-policing an important survival strategy. For women who do not occupy positions of privilege in relation to race, class, sexuality and health, concern about the judgements and reactions of others can offer self-protection by helping to detect or predict potentially denigrating or dangerous situations. In this sense, self-policing can be experienced as empowering.[11] Furthermore, any emphasis on the importance of women developing their own voices needs to be seen in the context of culturally elevated values of self-expression, independence and self-determination in western societies. These values constitute the yardstick frequently used to distinguish between emancipatory and oppressive practices. In other cultures, however, such values may not be privileged. Charles Waldegrave cites the example of a Pacific Islander living in New Zealand being asked the very common question "What do you think?" about a certain issue. He notes that for a Samoan such a question is alien and extremely intrusive. A response requires a tricky exercise in mental acrobatics to calculate a consensus of the thoughts of a range of family members (Waldegrave, 1998, p. 407). This example is a reminder that the appropriateness of an individualistic orientation towards resisting oppressive social practices cannot be assumed.

THE EFFECTS OF VIOLENCE AND ABUSE

In addition to the broad categories of class, race, sexuality, health, and so on, experiences of violence and abuse also can intensify self-policing. This involves heightened vulnerability to self-surveillance,[12] harsh self-judgements, insidious comparisons with the apparent normality of others, various self-negations and personal isolation. When this occurs an exposé of the broader cultural context is crucial. In a feminist therapeutic setting, this involves exploring culturally popular ideas about the abuse of girls and women which may be contributing to its ongoing legacy in a woman's life. This is particularly important in relation to sexual abuse because, in addition to the trauma of the actual abuse and manipulation from the abuser, the survivor also generates or is recruited into various meanings in relation to the abuse. These meanings are, in large part, informed by broader cultural beliefs about gender and power and the attribution of responsibility (O'Leary, 1998, p. 25). Such beliefs – for instance that girls or women must have led the perpetrator on or in some way provoked the abuse (for example by acting seductively, wearing certain clothing, being out late at night, being drunk) or that had they really wanted to they could have stopped the abuse/attack, and so forth – often reinforce feelings of self-blame and shame even though the abuse may have occurred in the relative powerlessness of childhood, or in adulthood in the terrifying context of rape and/or other forms of physical violence. The influence of these beliefs relies on denial of the power imbalances integral to abuse.

Contextualizing the effects of violence and abuse within broader cultural beliefs provides an opportunity for individuals to consider the personal impact of such beliefs (Kamsler, 1990, pp. 24–25). This has the potential to diminish self-blame and opens space for women to begin to appreciate more fully their ability to survive often horrendous circumstances. This, in turn, enables the charting of a personal history of resistance to the abuse and its ongoing effects, including those that continue to be reinforced by the broader culture. An awareness of the latter illuminates the enormity of what abuse survivors frequently are up against, which increases the possibility for an enhanced appreciation of their efforts. Out of this process a revision of the relationship with oneself becomes possible.[13] This permits a move away from the extremely negative stories of identity that are often part of the legacy of abuse (White, 1995, pp. 83–84, 86, 88–89). For some women this can include attempts to secure justice through confronting, reporting or legally charging the perpetrator. As mentioned earlier, it is also the case that women who have been subject to abuse are often surprised to learn that many women who have not been abused also struggle with disempowering voices of self-doubt, self-criticism and self-negation. This information can be relayed in a way that does not under-state the frequently more intense experiences of those whose lives have been subject to the trauma of abuse. Thus conveyed, it can help soften an often absolute sense of *otherness* experienced by some survivors. From a feminist perspective, this degree of commonality among women can be seen to reflect a link between the childhood sexual abuse of girls and intensified gender training:

> The child's interactions with the perpetrator can be described as "intensive training" for her in fitting with the stereotypical submissive female role. The groundwork has been thoroughly prepared for the woman to respond in strongly gendered ways in other significant relationships. She may begin habitually to apply the perpetrator's prescriptions to herself in numerous situations, e.g. putting her own needs aside and developing a "being for others" lifestyle in her relationships, being passive, being obedient. Thus, the effect of these interactions in childhood may be that she conforms even more strongly to gender prescriptions for women.[14]
>
> (Kamsler, 1990, pp. 18–19)

Finally, although I have pointed to the likelihood that the intensity of self-policing will vary among diverse groups of women, it is also important not to collapse intra-group difference. While women may share ethnicity, sexual orientation, class or experiences of violence and abuse, a variety of other intersecting influences can generate differences in relations with the self. Moreover, in addition to the likelihood that self-policing practices will differ among and within different groups of women, the extent to which they dominate individual self-relations can vary. If it is accepted that selves are constituted in a number of ways through various interactions with other persons, social practices, institutions and structures, then we can expect individual identities to be multivocal. In relation to self-policing this means that, while for some women such a practice may permeate self-relations generally, for others it may be limited to certain aspects of identity and experience. For instance, a woman may be critical or punitive towards herself regarding academic or career performance while being at ease with her parenting or friendship practices (or vice versa). Such variation is likely to reflect individual experience and circumstance. Hence a working-class background may preclude the sense of entitlement and confidence regarding study and career prospects that often is generated by a middle-class upbringing. Conversely, confident mothering can be fostered by a supportive and loving family environment regardless of class background. In this way, identity practices can be seen to cut across each other to form complex relations of power. Another example might be the piercing of middle-class confidence by the discriminating "gaze" of heterosexist culture. It also may be the case that self-policing features more strongly at particular times in the life cycle – for instance in relation to ageing in the context of youth and beauty standards of normalcy. Despite the fact that self-policing may not exert power in relation to some aspects of identity, its dominance over others may diminish awareness of this. When this is the case, identification of areas in which self-policing is absent or at a low level can help decrease its power in other areas. Moreover, even when much or all of the self-relationship is characterized by self-policing, instances of resistance always exist and can be mobilized in support of a renegotiated relationship. This type of strategy is elaborated in the following chapter.

SUMMARY

This chapter both draws on Foucault's analysis of self-policing and points to its limitations with regard to gender. In relation to women's lives, I pointed to certain common features – the legacy of secondary or inferior status and a frequent imbalance between caring for others and caring for the self – which are likely to reflect and heighten self-policing. I discussed a range of self-policing practices characteristic, to varying degrees, of many women's self-relationship. These include surveillance of one's thoughts, feelings and conduct, ongoing self-judgement, self-criticism, insidious comparisons with others and personal isolation. Such practices tend to be experienced as a given part of psychic make up which makes it difficult to subject them to critical scrutiny. Yet their disabling effects render this important. Foregrounding self-policing and examining the context in which it prospers undermines its seemingly inevitable status. In turn, this increases possibilities for developing a different type of self-relationship and for active participation in broader questions of identity.

Although self-policing is depicted as a common feature of women's lives, this is not intended to conflate differences among women. If self-governance ensures the measuring of individual worth in line with dominant identity prescriptions, its intensity is likely to be enhanced for those relegated to marginalized social locations. In addition to broad categories of race, class, sexuality and health, experiences of violence and abuse can render women vulnerable to heightened self-policing. At the same time, its degree and intensity can vary within groups and individuals.

The following chapter looks at a therapeutic approach capable of destabilizing the seeming inevitability of self-policing and facilitating the development of different self-relations and understandings. Nonetheless, the ideas and practices characterizing this approach need not be limited to the therapeutic context.

3

CHALLENGING NEGATIVE IDENTITY PRACTICES – NARRATIVE THERAPY

INTRODUCTION

This chapter introduces a therapeutic approach whose ethical and political framework is compatible with a feminist analysis of self-policing.[1] Central to this approach, commonly known as narrative therapy, is concern about the way in which oppressive practices and structures of the wider society might be being reproduced in the therapeutic environment. This leads it to reflect critically on a number of therapeutic realities and to develop practices which challenge an individualistic orientation to therapy and the idea of the therapist as objective expert. A key practice emerging out of narrative therapy is "externalization of the problem". Challenging the conventional notion of internal pathology, externalizing practices create space for people to actively intervene to diminish the influence of problems. This process can be aided by exploring historical, cultural and gender dimensions of problematic experience and personal histories of resistance. These practices pave the way for the development and performance of alternative, preferred stories of identity and relationship. Alternative narratives do not entail any notion of an innate or "true" self but rather emerge from an exploration of people's preferred values, beliefs and desires. Moreover, moving away from any notion of therapy as a purely individual pursuit, emphasis is placed on the important role played by others in authenticating and strengthening revised identity projects. In the final section of the chapter, I discuss the question of whether narrative therapy's location within poststructuralist thought renders it vulnerable to charges of moral relativism.

DIFFERENT SITES OF RESISTANCE

The entrenched nature of self-policing can result in its ongoing presence despite the existence of various institutional and attitudinal improvements in the social position of women. A similar point is made by Naomi Wolf in relation to many contemporary western women's concerns about their failure to measure up to prescribed notions of beauty, as reflected in the widespread incidence of eating disorders and use of cosmetic surgery (Wolf, 1992, pp. 9–12). Foucault's insistence on the need to study the effects of power at the "micro-physical" level of bodies, thoughts, wills, conduct and everyday lives of individuals is apposite here: "The overthrow of these 'micro-powers' . . . is not acquired once and for all by a new control of the apparatuses nor by a new functioning or a destruction of the institutions" (Foucault, 1979, p. 27). In other words, it is not enough to change governments or the workings of various institutions or social practices, important though this may be in movements for progressive social change. If the micro-level of life is ignored, a range of unwanted power relations will remain intact. This points to the importance of addressing power's hold at the intra-subjective level of women's self-relations as one part of the struggle for greater self-definition. One strategy for achieving this is to destabilize the idea that self-policing practices form an inevitable part of identity:

> In my experience, the hardest step is to become aware of the [self-critical] voices' insidious presence and notice them in our daily activities. Then, talking about them and looking at their effects is probably the most effective way of making them visible enough to take a stance against them. It is much easier to fight an enemy that you can see than one that is secretly glued onto you. After that, every single time you resist them, they lose their power over you.
>
> (Beaudoin in Dickerson, 1998, p. 44)

NARRATIVE THERAPY

One therapeutic approach compatible with a feminist exposé of self-policing is narrative therapy. Narrative therapy develops out of the collaborative work of Australian and New Zealand family therapists Michael White and David Epston during the 1980s. Significantly influenced by Foucault's thought, feminism and cultural anthropology, this approach is concerned about the ways in which various taken-for-granted therapeutic assumptions inadvertently may be reproducing oppressive practices or structures of the broader society and thus contributing to the very problems people are seeking to address. These include a predominantly individualistic approach to therapy which obscures the social context in which problems develop and prosper. Such an approach tends to ignore the link between personal identity and experience and the broader power structures of society. Conversely, narrative therapy is interested in the degree to which problematic experience is caught up in taken-for-granted cultural assumptions and structures of inequality (White, 1995, p. 115).

From this perspective, to ignore the impact of broader social structures can result in therapists inadvertently adjusting people to various forms of injustice. In one example, Charles Waldegrave points to the phenomenon of unemployment in western societies which can result in feelings of classic depression and other problematic symptoms. As he notes, this is not surprising as it frequently entails the lack of reasonable income, the lowly status of welfare recipient, a lack of social contact and structure provided by a workplace and feelings of guilt about not having a job or being able to provide adequately for one's family. He claims that in the therapeutic situation, if individualizing discourses about unemployment go unchallenged and clinical symptoms are treated purely as internal, personal or family problems, those seeking assistance frequently experience themselves and are perceived by others as individual failures. This reinforces the destructive myth that unemployed people are to blame for their situation. It fails to take into account the effects of largescale deregulation and restructuring in contemporary western economies which have resulted in structural unemployment in certain areas of the economy and among certain sections of the populace. In this light those thrown into unemployment, while the rest of society lives in relative prosperity, can be seen as casualties of a macro-economic plan rather than as instances of individual inadequacy (Waldegrave, 1990, pp. 23–24).

The power effects of individualizing discourses also are evident in relation to privileged conceptions of selfhood. As Foucault and others have noted, in modern western culture these increasingly have entailed notions of self-containment or self-possession. While this type of cultural prescription produces norms of independence and self-reliance around which individuals are incited to fashion their identities and lives, its ill-fitting nature can have tragic effects. One example given by White refers to his work with a man whose efforts to conform to such a prescription resulted in ongoing acts of self-torture during a long involvement in the psychiatric system:

> In his attempts to achieve a sense of moral worth in his community, he had been operating on his thoughts, his body, his lifestyle, his soul and so on. He had been doing all of this in the name of self-possession, self-containment, self-dependence and so on – nothing special you know, just the sort of specifications for personhood that are valorised in our culture.
> (Bubenzer *et al.*, 1994, p. 81)

This is a stark example of the disabling effects of given identity norms. Yet struggles to conform to such norms are not restricted to those in the psychiatric system. As noted, their social elevation produces a powerful incitement for individuals generally to measure themselves against uniform standards. As a result they are seen to "reflect degrees of inadequacy, abnormality, insufficiency, incompetency, hopelessness, ineffectualness, deficit, imperfection and worthlessness" (White, 2002, p. 43). This encourages a self-relationship in which our bodies, thoughts, desires and actions become objects for disciplinary and corrective procedures. In addition to the likely harsh and punitive character of such a relationship, this type of self-orientation effectively constrains the diverse range of possibilities for selfhood. While the effects of such a constraint are widespread, they are particularly pernicious for those designated society's "other".

A further target of narrative therapy's critique is the model of the therapist as expert. The following account of its resistance to such a model is not intended to imply uniqueness in this regard. Certain other therapies no doubt will recognize themselves in at least some of the practices outlined in the text that follows. The notion of expertise, common to a broad range of professional disciplines, derives from the belief that it is possible to gain access to an objective truth. The predominance of such a view is hardly surprising given the status of the scientific paradigm in modernity. Yet the perception of knowledge as neutral and universal discourages reflection on its concrete effects. In the therapeutic context, the imposition of expert knowledge claims about the formation and resolution of problematic experience can be profoundly disempowering. As Johnella Bird argues, this is not to downplay the importance of therapeutic knowledges, skills and experience but rather to highlight that what therapists cannot claim to know is the content of people's situated experience (Bird, 1999). Echoing such a view, narrative therapy sees those consulting therapists as best placed to be an authority on the effects of problems and the content of preferred ways of thinking and living (Freedman and Combs, 1996, p. 282). This means that the therapist "can't know, in advance, what's 'right' for people – can't even know how the family 'should' look at the end of therapy" (White, 1995, p. 66).

This type of orientation locates therapists at a position between knowing and not knowing which encourages receptivity to having their knowledge challenged, added to and/or affirmed (Bird, 2000, pp. ix, 12, 14, 22, 127). It also allows greater appreciation of the particularity of people's experience rather than any assumption that "one model fits all". Such an approach requires therapists to develop "radical listening" skills rather than being armed with various hypotheses and ideas about how to solve people's problems. Radical listening affords an entry point into the world of those seeking assistance (Weingarten, 1998, p. 5). Moreover, the onus is on the therapist to check regularly whether he or she has adequately understood people's description of their experience (White, 1991, p. 37). This type of collaboration is facilitated by a questioning style as opposed to making claims or offering observations in an authoritative tone or form. An example might be: "Well, I wonder if this experience could have played some part in this recent development, or do you think that it's entirely irrelevant to this?" (White, 1995, p. 30). Moreover, the type of language used is seen as crucial in determining whether the therapeutic interaction is felt to be respectful or discounting of people's experience (White, 1995, p. 30). The kind of orientation outlined should not diminish therapists' ability to engage with difficult issues that arise in therapy, for example those of self-harm or harm to others. Rather, seeking to understand the particularity of people's experience and the development of a collaborative, respectful relationship maximizes possibilities for effective engagement with the often complex, intricate, sometimes dangerous nature of problematic experience.

Once the idea of an objective account of reality is questioned, greater emphasis on therapists' responsibility for the concrete effects of their work becomes possible:

> Therapists can challenge the idea that they have an expert view by continually encouraging persons to evaluate the real effects of the therapy in their lives and relationships, and to determine for themselves to what extent these effects are preferred effects and to what extent they are not. The feedback that arises from this evaluation assists therapists to squarely face the moral and ethical implications of their practices.
>
> (White, 1991, p. 37)

In this way, therapists are encouraged to examine the values and beliefs informing their practices and the real effects of these. This type of accountability can be developed further by inviting people to interview the therapist about the ideas and experience informing her or his questions and responses. These then can be situated in the context of therapists' particular experience, knowledge, intentions and imagination. This increases the possibility of people deciding how they want to relate to these views rather than automatically accepting them as true (White, 1991, pp. 37–38).[2]

A further challenge to the expert model lies in the explicit acknowledgement of therapy as a two-way process. This counters any tendency towards a notion of the therapist as dispenser of the therapy and those seeking assistance as passive recipients. Such a notion is likely to encourage or reinforce the idea of those seeking therapy as "other" or "less than" (White, 1995, p. 168; 1997, pp. 120, 127–129). Moreover, it diminishes the likelihood of therapists gaining information that may be useful for an understanding of people's particular problems and which, in turn, may contribute to greater effectiveness in work with others. Even if this does happen, the idea of the therapist as expert may discourage its acknowledgement. Narrative therapy's approach to the therapeutic inter-action is not, however, just a question of the exchange of knowledge. It also refers to the gift of

> inspiration that we experience in this work as we witness persons changing their lives despite formidable odds, and as we experience the real effects of this in our lives; [and] the contribution that others make to the sustenance of our vision, and of our commit-ment to this work.
>
> (White, 1994a, p. 3)

It is held further that seeking to understand a person's experience in their own terms, and collaborating in their process of change, holds the promise of transformation in the life of therapists, enabling "us to extend on the limits of our thinking, and to fill some of the gaps in our own self-narratives" (White, 1994a, p. 3). If one does not know the "truth" about people's lives, there are a myriad of possibilities for learning and being changed in the therapeutic interaction, both professionally and personally. For White, acknowledging these benefits can help minimize the inherent power imbalance in the therapeutic relationship (White, 1997, pp. 131–142).

THE NARRATIVE METAPHOR

As implied in the name of this approach, it is informed by the metaphor of narrative. This refers to the cultural narratives or stories through which individuals gain a sense of identity and a way of interpreting or under-standing life events. These stories reflect the values, beliefs and customs that have gained prominence in a culture at a particular historical point. Thus while they are usually presented as the "right" way to live, they are nonetheless specific historical constructions:

> These knowledges are not about discoveries regarding the "nature" of persons and of relationships, but are constructed knowledges that are specifying of a particular strain of personhood and of relationship. For example, in regard to dominant knowledges of personhood, in the West these establish a highly individual and gender distinct specification for ways of being in the world.
>
> (White, 1991, pp. 28–29)

In the narrative therapeutic account, although these cultural stories struc-ture our identities and lives they can never capture the full complexity of

47

lived experience. What tends to remain unstoried are those experiences that lie beyond culturally favoured interpretations. It is in trying to make sense of the various gaps, contradictions and ambiguities between narratives and lived experience that the imaginative capacity of individuals is invoked. In this process we enter into stories, re-authoring them as our own and thus actively participate in the shaping of our lives (White and Epston, 1990, pp. 11–13). As two practitioners of narrative therapy explain:

> A key to this therapy is that in any life there are always more events that don't get "storied" than there are ones that do – even the longest and most complex autobiography leaves out more than it includes. This means that when life narratives carry hurtful meanings or seem to offer only unpleasant choices, they can be changed by highlighting different, previously un-storied events or by taking new meaning from already-storied events, thereby constructing new narratives. Or, when dominant cultures carry stories that are oppressive, people can resist their dictates and find support in subcultures that are living different stories.
>
> (Freedman and Combs, 1996, pp. 32–33)

Clearly, the capacity to intervene in one's life is less available to some groups than others. As noted, hierarchical structures of domination and subordination are reflected in social divisions of race, class, gender, sexuality, health, and so on. Because of the very real effects of such structures on the constitution of meaning in people's lives, the narrative metaphor is extended to incorporate an understanding of the crucial link between notions of selfhood and the broader power structures of society (White, 1995, pp. 66–67). This results in the development of therapeutic practices that assist people to disturb the taken-for-granted nature of cultural stories that have come to dominate and oppress them – for instance the common belief that problems reflect individual pathology or that women are wholly responsible for the emotional well-being of families, or the idea that dominant identity specifications of self-possession and self-responsibility rule out a need to consider the broader context in which problems arise. Holding such notions up for critical scrutiny is important because the influence of problems often is reinforced and perpetuated by people's firm belief in the culturally accepted description of their experience, thus disqualifying or neglecting their own local understandings about their lives (Madigan, 1992, p. 273). The deconstruction of singular understandings paves the way for "the identification or generation of alternative stories that enable [people] to perform new meanings, bringing with them desired possibilities – new meanings that persons will experience as more helpful, satisfying, and open-ended" (White and Epston, 1990, p. 15). These new meanings emerge from the often neglected or inarticulated aspects of lived experience that lie beyond culturally dominant understandings (Freedman and Combs, 1996, pp. 39–40).

EXTERNALIZING THE PROBLEM

Central to narrative therapy is a perception that the problems people experience constitute the basis of what needs to be dealt with in the therapeutic situation. While this sounds like a truism, it is a key feature of the approach aimed at countering any conflation of the person and the problem which extends the notion of pathology to the whole person. The latter has the effect of totalizing a person's identity as in the case of "the manic depressive", "the schizophrenic" or "the anorexic". When this occurs, aspects of identity which lie outside the problems experienced tend to go unrecognized. In addition to the negative effects this is likely to have on a person's sense of self, it also neglects aspects of identity which can be mobilized to counter problematic experience. It is in opposition to this type of totalization that narrative therapy depicts the problem, rather than the person, as the problem. This enables people to conceive of the problem as in some sense external to them.

This process is facilitated by engaging people in "externalizing conversations" about the ways in which their lives and relationships have been affected by the problem. In so doing special emphasis is given to how the problem has people seeing themselves and their relationships with others, and the influence of these perceptions in various areas of their lives – for example, "How does the depression have you feeling and thinking about yourself, how does it have you viewing your relationships with other family members/friends/workmates? What impact do these ways of thinking and feeling have on your relationship with yourself, with others, on your parenting, your work?" This type of enquiry reveals what White refers to as the "problem-saturated" account of a person's life which is much broader than the account commonly offered of the problem itself. In addition to identifying disabling practices of the self and relationship, it also becomes possible to acknowledge the degree to which people have been trained into policing their own lives, as well as ways in which they may have been participating in policing the lives of others. In this way, practices which support and reinforce the "life" of the problem are pinpointed. This exploratory process can be extended to trace the history of certain "truths" people have held about themselves – for example, "When you think back over your life, can you recall where this idea about you being a depressed person came from? Who or what has provided support for or reinforced such a notion?" This enables discovery of how they were

49

recruited into a particular story about who they are and the practices associated with such a story (White, 1991, pp. 29, 35–36; 1995, pp. 21, 24; White and Epston, 1990, pp. 42–43).

In taking this approach, narrative therapy is running up against a common phenomenon whereby people have internalized a belief that they are the problem. Although it is frequently unhelpful in overcoming problems, such an attitude is compatible with the entrenched belief in individual responsibility in much of western culture. As noted earlier, while there is certainly a sense in which taking responsibility for our lives fits with a notion of human agency and choice, the emphasis on personal responsibility frequently obscures the social context in which problems occur. This can result in individuals feeling responsible for factors that are completely beyond their control and issues of social justice are left unaddressed. Aware that therapeutic discourses are just as vulnerable to incorporating taken-for-granted cultural assumptions about people's moral worth as those who consult therapists are, narrative therapy consciously explores the context in which personal struggles emerge and flourish. At times this involves exploring with people the effects of inequitable social structures. Thus while people's stories are of personal struggle and triumph they are also stories of local relationship politics and of broader cultural politics of race, gender, class, sexuality and professional and institutional dominance (Wylie, 1994, p. 44). Contextualizing problems relieves people of the heavy burden of self-blame so they are more easily able to appreciate the hurdles they have been up against in their lives and to recognize and value the ways in which they have resisted problematic experience, often in the face of considerable adversity.

As this suggests, externalizing often requires a conceptual shift. Asking questions which posit the problem as separate from the person destabilizes the common belief that problems reflect internal pathology: "Through externalizing conversations, the problem is to an extent disempowered, as it no longer speaks to persons of the truth about who they are as people, or about the very nature of their relationships" (White, 1995, p. 23). This helps people to begin to separate from an habitual reading of the problem and to experience a new sense of personal agency. Once this occurs, a revision of their relationship with the problem becomes possible (White and Epston, 1990, pp. 39–41). This also can pave the way for everyone involved with the problem to unite in standing against it in order to undermine its influence in their lives and relationships (White, 1988/9, p. 6). In White's experience, externalizing conversations which map the influence of the problem may need to be quite extensive when the problem has a particularly strong hold. He gives the example of young women whose lives have been taken over by anorexia nervosa and who are convinced of the need to carry out various disciplinary operations on their bodies, thoughts and souls in order to experience a legitimate way of being.

In addition to exposing the tactics, purposes and effects of anorexia, externalizing practices can assist women to identify and challenge cultural practices that objectify women's bodies in line with certain prescriptions for authenticity. When problems do not exert such a strong grip on people's lives, however, externalizing conversations may not be a necessary forerunner to re-storying. For instance, some people may be seeking assistance in relation to a particular crisis and others may have alternative self and relationship narratives relatively close at hand. Nonetheless, re-storying work itself deconstructs the dominant stories that have overshadowed the preferred account of people's lives (White, 1995, pp. 23–24; White and Epston, 1990, pp. 75–76).

RESPONSIBILITY

Given that those seeking therapeutic assistance often contribute to the ongoing life of problems and that some also engage in the oppression of others, one criticism is that externalizing practices encourage the abdication of personal responsibility. Such a claim is refuted, however, on the basis that it is precisely the highlighting of people's relationship with the problem that enables them to take a responsibility hitherto unavailable. When people recognize their relationship with the problem, a renegotiation of that relationship becomes possible: "When a problem defines someone, there is little she can do about it. It is her. When a problem is external to a person, she can take responsibility for how she interacts with it" (Freedman and Combs, 1996, p. 63). In this way, externalization encourages a sense of personal agency which allows responsibility to be taken for the exploration of new choices and possibilities (White and Epston 1990, p. 65). Conversely when problems are internalized personal agency often is diminished. Externalizing the problem, moreover, does not diminish responsibility for the abuse of others. In such instances, it is not abuse or violence that is externalized but rather the attitudes and beliefs that seem to compel the abuse, and tactics such as secrecy and isolation practices (White 1988/9, p. 8). This creates space for people to adopt a position on the familiar and taken-for-granted practices of power they have been engaging in and stand against their influence (for example see White, 1991, pp. 25–26).[3] Alan Jenkins notes that, in contrast to this type of approach, dominant and popular psychology models tend to perceive violence and abuse either in terms of "madness" or "badness", both of which work against the acceptance of personal responsibility:

> "Madness" models construct violence and abuse as symptoms of some form of pathology, either at an individual, family, developmental, or socio-cultural level. "Badness" models generally focus

51

on concepts of individual deviance. Both sets of explanation foster preoccupations with limitations and deficits, and a sense of individual insufficiency and incapacity. Both create considerable obstacles to individuals accepting responsibility for their actions and developing more respectful behaviour. Causal explanations become excuses, and justifications are more often used to explain why change and responsible behaviour are not possible.

(Jenkins, 1994, p. 15)

Following the exploration of the problem's influence in a person's life, a revision of their relationship with the problem can be facilitated through a charting of their own influence. As with the idea of the problem influencing the person, the notion of the person influencing the problem establishes the idea of people having a relationship with the problem rather than them *being* the problem (Freedman and Combs, 1996, p. 66). The mapping of a personal history of resistance to problems elicits information that contradicts the problem-saturated account of people's lives and helps them identify their skills and competence in adverse circumstances (White, 1988/9, p. 6).[4]

UNIQUE OUTCOMES

In his work with a young woman whose life was in the grip of anorexia nervosa, White notes that

it was only after mapping the influence of anorexia nervosa in her life and upon her relationships that [she] was able to appreciate the profound significance in the fact that she had not allowed the problem to isolate her from friends.

(White, 1988/9, p. 7)

Following Irving Goffman, this type of contradiction is referred to as a "unique outcome". Unique outcomes can encompass the whole range of experience, emotions, thoughts, intentions, actions and desires in the past, present or future that stand outside the dominant (problematic) story. They provide an entry-point to the alternative, preferred story of people's lives. While their presence can never be forecast from the problem-saturated account of a person's life, they always exist (White and Epston, 1990, pp. 15–16). A painfully poignant example is reflected in one young woman's experience of childhood sexual abuse:

After my father would rape and beat me, I would wait until he left the room. Then I would stand up. I would never let him totally win. There was a part of my inner-being, my spirit, that would never agree with what was happening to me. I couldn't stand up while he was there – it would have been too dangerous. He would have beaten me again. But once it was safe, I stood up. There was a part of me he could never get to – my hope. I knew there were other ways of treating children, that this abuse was not justified – that it would never be. Speaking about these acts of resistance, sharing them together has made a real difference.

(Silent Too Long, 1998b, p. 5)

Once a unique outcome is identified, people are encouraged to reflect on the meaning this holds for them. Other instances of refusing to perform in line with the problem's requirements then can be identified and connected to give an historical account of resistance to the problem. Historicizing unique outcomes intensifies the significance of current acts of resistance. People also can be invited to speculate about further possibilities for defiance and how these might impact on their lives and relationships. Out of this process there starts to develop an alternative history. Reflecting on alternative histories enables people to gain a clear sense of their preferred values and commitments (White and Epston, 1990, pp. 31–32, 41; White, 1995, p. 26). This process is facilitated by questions that help to identify both the concrete acts of resistance over time and the meaning people attribute to these. Some examples of such questions might be: "When you think back over your life, are there any events which would lead you not to be surprised at your ability to take this recent step?" "Let's reflect for a moment on these recent developments. What new conclusions might you reach about your tastes; about what is appealing to you; about what you are attracted to?" (White, 1991, pp. 30–31). Other questions can invite people to reflect on what they imagine someone else's experience of them might be, for example: "If I had been a spectator to your life when you were a younger person, what do you think I might have witnessed you doing then that might help me to understand how you were able to achieve [this latest step]? . . . Of all those persons who have known you, who would be least surprised that you have been able to take this step . . .? What might they have [known about you] that would have made it possible for them to predict that you could take such a step at this point in your life?" (White, 1991, p. 32).

In investigating instances of resistance it is important to remember that, while the therapist can ask questions which privilege previously ignored aspects of experience, only those consulting the therapist can determine what comprises a unique outcome. Thus White notes that something that might be insignificant in the life of the therapist, such as welcoming a visitor to one's home, may be a highly significant feat to someone else – "perhaps equivalent to the therapist taking a walk on a tightrope" (White,

1988/9, p. 14). Once a unique outcome is identified as meaningful, the role of the therapist is to facilitate the development of an alternative story in line with a person's preferred desires, values, beliefs and intentions. Thus while re-storying requires the active participation of everyone involved in the therapeutic process, a concerted effort is made to privilege family members as the primary authors. In this way, re-storying does not involve the therapist coming up with a new and better account of people's lives (White, 1991, p. 30; 1995, p. 66). This type of approach is compatible with a feminist commitment to encouraging women's own description of their experience and desires in contrast to the historical practice of being spoken for by others.

NON-ESSENTIAL IDENTITY

The development of alternative narratives, moreover, does not involve a search for universally applicable meanings: "The development of a preferred self-description involves a choice of what facts we decide to privilege in the meaning that we make of our lives, not a search for what are the true and only facts" (Law, 1998b, p. 192). Re-authoring work, therefore, does not entail the uncovering of a "true" or "deep" self which has been repressed by personal, familial or sociohistorical constraints. Rather it involves exploring people's identification with cultural values, beliefs and aspirations they prefer over those which historically have shaped their inherited story of identity. Non-essentialist notions of selfhood open space for creative self-making and, in encouraging an understanding of identity as fluid, leave open the possibility of further self-experimentation. This approach importantly challenges the practice of evaluating people in line with privileged understandings about human nature. In White and Epston's experience, this type of practice often reproduces the very problems with which people are struggling (White, 1997, pp. 54–55, 231–232). This is not to advocate an "anything goes" approach but rather to encourage the transgression of current limits to more inclusive, open-ended identity-making.

THE SIGNIFICANCE OF OTHERS

Narrative therapy emphasizes the crucial role played by "outsider witnesses" in legitimating new self-understandings. The need to involve others in such projects becomes self-evident when considering the significant role played by so many (families, schools, church, media, legal system, peers, etc.) in the original process of identity formation: "If the stories that we have about [our] lives are negotiated and distributed within communities of persons, then it makes a great deal of sense to engage communities of persons in the renegotiation of identity" (White, 1995, p. 26). In the therapeutic context, this occurs through the recruitment of supportive audiences which reinforce and strengthen new meanings thereby increasing their availability for performance in daily life. A parallel can be seen here with the feminist emphasis on the need for solidarity among women in facilitating the development of different identities. In narrative therapy, one method of enlisting an audience is through assisting people to regenerate associations of love and support from which they have been dis-membered by the dominance of problematic experience. Such "re-membering" practices can include reclaiming previous links to supportive family members and friends (as well as to past interests/hobbies) and aspects of the self obscured by the problem. It also can entail connecting people to new forms and communities of support. This allows people to have a greater say about whose voices should be authorized to speak on matters of their identity, and links them to shared values, beliefs and commitments. This process can be facilitated by interviewing people known to the person consulting the therapist in their presence. Sometimes these people may have been out of contact with the person attending therapy for a long period. The therapist can ask what they remember about the person that might throw light on their ability to have taken a recent step towards preferred ways of being. For the person attending therapy, experiencing past aspects of the self through the eyes of others helps strengthen the sense of a history of resistance to problematic experience, often in difficult circumstances. Moreover, acknowledging the importance of the past role played by the person(s) being interviewed generally allows those attending therapy to experience a richer description of their life. A further contribution to the legitimation of preferred stories can be made through therapeutic letters and documents which specifically refer to those comprising an appropriate audience; these also can be shown to others in order to enlist them in the person's re-authoring project. Re-membering practices generally enable people to experience the fuller presence of audience members in their daily lives even when they are no longer living, or close by (White, 1995, pp. 27, 143; 1997, pp. 23, 61).

Another type of audience to re-authored stories can be found in "reflecting teamwork". This involves a group of therapists (and/or others) carefully listening to, discussing and extending the original story of those attending therapy in ways that help enrich the description of their identities and lives. Various structures of transparency and accountability are built into this process. There is also acknowledgement of the often trans-formative effects routinely experienced by team members as they bear witness to people's struggles and triumphs, often in circumstances in which they cannot imagine doing so well themselves (White, 1995, pp. 172–198; 1999, pp. 55–82).

Emphasis on the important role played by others in re-authoring work further challenges an individualist approach to therapy. For Epston and White such a conception, based on the broader cultural ethos of individualism, tends to separate therapy from a person's everyday community, which can lead to problems when therapy ends. This type of conception informs the predominant "termination-as-loss" metaphor in therapeutic literature. They see this as reflecting a privileging of the therapeutic relationship and a view of termination as requiring the person(s) to adjust to making it on their own. Conversely, narrative therapy depicts the final stages of therapy as a celebration of new beginnings in which a person(s) rejoins others in a familiar social environment, and is encouraged to invite others to celebrate and acknowledge their arrival at a preferred place in life (Epston and White, 1990, pp. 27–28).

MORAL RELATIVISM

In this final section, I look at the issue of moral relativism. Charges of moral relativism reflect concern that, if there are no overarching or universal values beyond particular sociohistorical constructions of human life, it is impossible to distinguish the merits of different perspectives or stories about life – for example between a fascist and a democratic narrative. Poststructural or postmodern schools of thought are often the focus of such concern. As narrative therapy explicitly locates itself within poststructuralism, this issue needs to be addressed. In the development of narrative therapy, poststructuralist ideas provide a powerful framework for critiquing some of the key assumptions of dominant psychological theories, in particular the reproduction of broader cultural notions of an essential self (White, 1997, pp. ix, 119–120, 217–218, 222–223, 228). There also are commonly accepted beliefs about the nature of the authentic self – "about humanity, human development, identity formation, the workings of the psyche, and so on" (White, 1997, p. 119). Structuralist perspectives, for example, are informed by a surface/depth metaphor which reflects the assumption that beneath the external behaviour of individuals lie deeper systems of meaning which can be accessed, understood and treated by therapists. Another example is functionalism. This derives from biological theory and tends to perceive symptoms exhibited by people as a reaction to some other cause and as serving an essential function in a system. For instance, a child's disruptive behaviour may be understood as enhancing the closeness between parents. In family therapy, the influence of human nature metanarratives is reflected in the dominant organizing ideas of structuralism and functionalism. As Ian Law and Stephen Madigan note, structural and functional approaches require therapists to adopt positions of expert knowledge and language in order to help formulate, clarify, explain and treat symptoms. Such knowledge and language are based on the medical model which is characterized by deficit-language. This results in people and their problems being described and diagnosed in "less than" terms such as depression, disability, schizophrenia, incapacity, dysfunctional family, damaged, absence of intimacy, personality disorder, incompetence, and so forth (Law and Madigan, 1998, pp. 4–5). Moreover, the "truth" of these knowledges is seen to hold regardless of race, culture, gender, class, circumstance, and so on. For White, poststructural thought enables an examination of the concrete effects of these truth claims and associated practices of living (White, 1997, pp. 119, 222–223).

While it often is alleged that a poststructural framework is unable to provide any basis for making ethical judgements, the debate about moral relativism tends to suffer from the dichotomous approach characterizing much of modern thought. Once a less polarizing approach is adopted, however, it becomes possible to think about both constructive and dis-advantageous aspects of relativism within a single approach. Such a notion is reflected in Rachel Hare-Mustin's argument that a postmodern claim for epistemological relativism – the view that the infusion of all knowledge with values makes it impossible to determine the ultimate truth of any claim – need not lead to an "anything goes" position but rather "should propel us into dialogue about values and ethics, about what is good in human life and important in public philosophy" (Hare-Mustin, 1994, p. 32). She claims that because discourses incorporate the values and mores of daily life that construct our shared understandings, social constructionism is rooted in the ethical. This is not, however, an ethics whose authority is based on its transcendence of the particulars of daily life. From a post-modern perspective, judgements about discursive practices rest on their purpose and ethical implications rather than their truth value (Hare-Mustin, 1994, pp. 31–32). Such a view echoes Foucault's claim that genealogical investigations do not seek to determine the truth or falsity of various scientific discourses but rather to investigate the power effects of their truth status (Gordon, 1980, p. 84).

Engaged in precisely this type of enquiry, narrative therapy can be seen as epistemologically, but not morally, relativist. Its position is similar to that articulated by Ian Parker in relation to critical psychology. Parker describes critical psychology as relativizing traditional psychology's normative assumptions about human nature at the same time as resisting the relativization of moral critiques.[5] This type of approach enables the contestation of a discipline's so-called facts or assumptions whose given nature hitherto has placed them outside the bounds of legitimate question-ing (Parker, 1999a, p. 5). In a similar vein, White rejects any suggestion that this kind of epistemological relativism in narrative therapy extends to the ethical domain. For him, an approach which lays no claim to universal truth *increases* rather than decreases moral responsibility:

If we acknowledge that it is the stories that have been negotiated about our lives that make up or shape or constitute our lives, and if in therapy we collaborate with persons in the further negotiation or renegotiation of the stories of persons' lives, then we really are in a position of having to face and to accept, more than ever, a responsibility for the real effects of our interactions on the lives of others. We are confronted with a degree of responsibility in the assessment of the real effects of altered or alternative self-narratives.

(White, 1995, p. 15)

In this way, the absence of universal truth claims can lessen the likelihood of certain conceptions about human life attaining an untouchable quality which can serve to obscure the full range of their implications, including ones that may be abusive – as for example in culture- or gender-blind conceptions of the family (Seigfried, 1989, p. 67). The type of ethics encouraged by such an approach is one which "values the experience of people at the margins of any dominant culture or at the bottom of any culture's hierarchies and takes a strong ethical stance in favour of making space for such people's voices to be heard, understood, and responded to" (Freedman and Combs, 1996, p. 266). This echoes Foucault's belief that theoretical pluralism, as opposed to grand theory, enables "a redefinition and redescription of experience from the perspectives of those who are more often simply objects of theory" (Sawicki, 1991, p. 47). Taking responsibility for the concrete effects of interactions with those seeking assistance and a concern for the marginalized in society are two instances of narrative therapy taking a clear moral position.

A further example of the epistemological, but not ethical, relativism characterizing this approach can be seen in its view of the self. As Jill Freedman and Gene Combs argue, the diversity of cultural understandings of the self points to the fallacy of the view that there is an essential self immune to the dictates of time and space. For instance, there is considerable difference between the western conception of a self as individualized, self-contained and having depth and the Balinese notion of self "as a character in a timeless, unchanging drama" (Freedman and Combs, 1996, p. 34). Different selves emerge intersubjectively across and within specific cultural contexts and particular conceptions of the self gain dominance at certain historical moments. Yet the notion of diverse selves does not have to lead to a morally relativist position. Rather it can encourage examination of how particular constructions of the self have come about and their impact on our lives and those of others. In turn, this can lead to reflection on, and possible revision of, our commitments (Freedman and Combs, 1996, pp. 34–35). In this way, the view that there are multiple selves, multiple stories, multiple truths "makes it *more* necessary to examine our constructions and to decide carefully how to act on them, not less" (Freedman and Combs, 1996, p. 35).

While efforts to ascertain the ethical implications of particular self and life understandings clearly involve certain value positions, this does not require taking a position beyond culture. As Alexander Nehamas points out, it merely entails stepping outside the particular practice under review:

> We acquire our beliefs, our desires, our values at different times, in different circumstances, from various sources. Each one of us belongs to a number of distinct but overlapping communities, and each community has its own but overlapping standards of rationality . . . We don't need to stand outside *everything* in order to criticize and evaluate the standards and practices, the "reason," of any particular community. All we need is a position outside *it*. This position is provided by the many other communities of which we are all members.
>
> (Nehamas, 1988, pp. 34–35)

Such a notion is reflected in White's claim that "many of the taken-for-granted practices of the culture of psychotherapy that are reproductive of problematic aspects of . . . dominant culture" (White, 1995, p. 46) may be rendered transparent by stepping into alternative cultural sites: "We can explore the alternative modes of life and of thought that are associated with these alternative sites of culture. We can solicit critical feedback from persons of other races, cultures and classes" (White, 1995, p. 46).

The values underpinning narrative therapy's critique of psychotherapy parallel those motivating Foucault's critique of modern systems of thought. For Epston and White, Foucault's concern about the normative turning into the normalizing assumes a very real significance based on many years of practice in the mainstream psychiatric system and broader therapeutic community. As noted, in their experience the evaluation of therapeutic consumers according to dominant conceptions of human nature and associated practices of living often reproduces the very problems with which people are struggling (see White, 1995, p. 34). For this reason, narrative therapy makes a distinction between "values . . . based on foundational premises and on universal notions of the 'good' and ones that help to challenge abuse, domination, exploitation, cruelty, neglect, and so forth" (White, 1994b, p. 3).

Therapeutic approaches which emphasize ethical responsibility in relation to an objective reality would seem to be underpinned by a universal notion of the bad. This is reflected in narrative therapy's identification of values that help to challenge abuse, domination, exploitation, and so on. Such behaviours it would seem are always bad. This belief is based on empirical knowledge of their impoverishing effects. Moreover, while universal conceptions of a pre-discursive human nature are eschewed, as in Foucault's later work there is an a priori good of (non-essentialist) self-definition. Thus narrative therapy's commitment to what is morally bad is contingent on its prior sense of what is good. The things it defines as bad are so because of its primary commitment to assisting people to have a greater say in fashioning their identities. Anything that damages that is *ipso facto* bad. If dominatory expressions of living do constitute a universal "bad", this precludes self-definitions informed by notions of domination, cruelty, abuse, and so forth. In Chapter 4, I advocate this type of relationship to ethics in work which seeks to diminish the influence of self-policing.

SUMMARY

This chapter has outlined a therapeutic approach commonly referred to as narrative therapy. Central to this approach is concern about the way in which taken-for-granted therapeutic understandings inadvertently may be replicating oppressive practices and structures of the broader society and thus contributing to the very problems people are seeking to address. One of the key suspects is the individualizing discourse of western society which, in the therapeutic environment, encourages the idea of internal pathology and tends to obscure the social context within which prob-lematic experience occurs. There is also a challenge to the idea of the therapist as holder of objective truth about people's problems and the solutions to these. One of the key practices of narrative therapy is "externalization of the problem". Externalizing conversations assist people to separate from the common idea that problems are internal to them. This creates space to explore their relationship to problematic experience and the ways in which they may be both participating in, and resisting, it. This process also encourages exploration of the degree to which the problems people experience are caught up in unjust social structures. The charting of a history of personal resistance indicates the extent to which the problem has not got the better of people (often a surprise), and provides encouragement for ongoing resistance. It also offers clues to their preferred values, attributes and aspirations which provide the basis for an alternative self-description. The latter is authenticated and enriched by "outsider witnesses". Rather than reflecting the recovery of an innate self, re-authored narratives always evolve in relation to the sociohistorical context. The idea of relational identity encourages individual creativity and leaves open the possibility of further self-making. Finally, it was argued that while this approach adopts an epistemologically relativist position in relation to the taken-for-granted assumptions of its discipline, it is not morally relativist.

The ideas and practices informing narrative therapy promise to be helpful in the exploration and transformation of women's self-policing.[6] While not advocating it as the only possible approach or denying an overlap between some of its aspects and those of other therapies, the key features I perceive to be useful include: a respectful and acknowledging orientation towards those seeking assistance; an ethos of critical reflection towards taken-for-granted therapeutic assumptions; the development of practices which aim to counter the universalizing tendency of modern thought; a focus on the link between personal identity and the broader power structures of society; an emphasis on people's *relationship* with problems and the charting of personal histories of resistance; the re-storying of problematic aspects of identity in line with people's preferred values and aspirations; the notion of non-essential identity; and the enrichment of alternative narratives by supportive others who participate in their telling and re-telling. In order to optimize possibilities for the effective performance of the notion of relational identity advocated in this approach, I have found it useful to incorporate aspects of certain immanent critiques. This is taken up in the next chapter.

4

IMMANENT CRITIQUES: EXPANDED POSSIBILITIES FOR REFUSING SELF-POLICING

INTRODUCTION

The influence of narrative therapy particularly in countries such as Australia, New Zealand, Canada, the USA (and more recently the UK) has increased steadily over the last decade and a half. It has been applied creatively to a broad range of issues both in and beyond the traditional therapeutic context – for instance, it has been used by some indigenous communities in Australia to address issues of loss and injustice associated with aboriginal deaths in custody (see Reclaiming Our Stories . . ., 1995). It also has been used in the classroom context (see Dickerson, 1998, pp. 32–34) and in relation to management and business practices (White, 2000, p. 93). One therapist, moreover, points to its practical application with regard to her parenting practices and her personal life generally (Weingarten, 1998, pp. 5, 13–14; see White, 1997, *passim*). White sees its appeal as lying in the development of a framework which articulates, and provides the basis for extending, the values and preferred ways of working of many therapists (White, 1995, p. 63). Not surprisingly, narrative therapy also has attracted critics. For the present purposes, this chapter focuses on certain strands of critique by practitioners sympathetic to some aspects of this approach yet troubled by others. The most systematic of these comes from Johnella Bird. While sharing much of the ethical and political framework of narrative therapy (Bird, 2000, ix), Bird claims that an emphasis on the problem as separate from the person in externalization practices linguistically reinforces the conventional notion of an autonomous, pre-social self. This undermines narrative therapy's commitment to the notion of identity as always socially and historically constructed. Bird posits an alternative notion of "relational externalizing" as a more effective way of enacting the idea of non-essential selfhood. This type of linguistic mechanism promises to be useful in destabilizing the idea of self-policing as a fixed, inevitable part of identity and in facilitating the development of a preferred self-relationship. In the final part of the chapter, I look at some common pitfalls that may be experienced in efforts to diminish self-policing, and signal the subversive potential of friendship with the self.

CHAMPIONING INDIVIDUALISM?

Prior to discussing the usefulness of Bird's notion of relational externalizing, several other strands of immanent critique are discussed. One strand points to the apparent paradox between narrative therapy's depiction of western notions of individualism and personal autonomy as tyrannical measures of moral worth and the fact that those seeking therapy seem to characterize this approach precisely in terms of its fostering of "a freer, more robust feeling of personal agency and individual identity" (Wylie, 1994, p. 46). Although this may seem contradictory, what motivates narrative therapy's (and Foucault's) critique of dominant identity practices is their universal and restrictive prescriptions. I have referred in previous chapters to the disempowering effects of this. In exploring with people the impact of trying to measure up to dominant notions of identity, narrative therapy creates a space in which disabling effects can be challenged and engagement with preferred ways of being encouraged. For some people the embracing or strengthening of non-dominant identity practices may involve forging stronger connections to a particular community and a corresponding shift away from the more conventional view of freedom as independence from others. Various communities or sub-cultures provide a powerful site of resistance and support in the struggle for greater self-definition by culturally marginalized groups. At the same time, the importance of solidarity in oppositional groups can lead to a diminution of personal autonomy through the replacement of one essentialist notion of identity by another. This was one of Foucault's concerns about the "coming out" imperatives of movements like Gay Liberation. Although a strong supporter of such movements publicly, he pointed to the way in which the assumption of a more or less fixed sexual identity tends to close off possibilities for ongoing creative relationships with the self (Miller, 1994, pp. 255–257). Concern about the limiting effects of essentialism in socially progressive movements is echoed in contemporary feminist debate (see Butler, 1990b).

Another example of the way in which discourses of liberation can perpetuate existing constraints can be seen in Self-Help and New-Age philosophies which emphasize taking responsibility for one's life, creating one's own reality, finding one's true self, and so forth. This type of exclusive focus on individual responsibility and essentialism sits comfortably within dominant western identity practices. This no doubt explains, in part, their popular resonance. Nonetheless, like the dominant notions of individualism they mirror, these philosophies tend to erase the social context within which individual lives are shaped and encourage people to assume responsibility for aspects of existence beyond their control. This, in turn, creates vulnerability to a sense of failure in the likely event that certain constraints cannot be overcome. Rachel Hare-Mustin and Jeanne Marecek note that most of the self-help literature produced by feminist psychologists targets women and, regardless of intent, typically reinforces commonly accepted gender beliefs. These include the idea of women as more emotionally troubled than men and the belief that women are responsible for making relationships work and for generally taking care of the emotional needs of others. It also promotes the idea that individual effort alone can improve a woman's well-being (Hare-Mustin and Marecek, 1994, p. 18). In a therapeutic situation, when such philosophies have generated a sense of over-responsibility or personal failure, their deconstruction is important. This can entail asking questions which help to illuminate the ways in which personal beliefs and experience are con-strained and shaped by societal, economic and familial forces. Such an enquiry challenges the idea that the individual alone determines meaning. This opens space for an exploration of the aspects of self-help philosophies likely to assist identified goals and those unlikely to do so. Such an approach echoes Foucault's recognition that emancipatory discourses can embody hidden coercion through the reproduction of taken-for-granted ways of being in the name of psychological liberation (Foucault, 1978). In sum, it is not that narrative therapy rejects notions of individualism and personal autonomy per se but rather it challenges the truth status of dominant interpretations of these notions. This reflects the view that selves are constituted in a diversity of ways. Such a view opposes the depiction in conventional psychoanalytic theory of a fundamental sense of identity constituted in early childhood and continuing into adulthood regardless of socially constructed divisions (McNay, 1992, p. 9).

OPPOSITIONAL DISCOURSES

In and beyond the therapeutic context, drawing a distinction between challenging the dominant status of discourses and privileging alternative ways of being is crucial to avoid reproducing the cultural practice of imposing truth. It is the truth status of identity practices which devalues or silences other possible options. Deprived of such a status they lose this type of power. Instead we could imagine the existence of communities in which negotiation about certain shared meanings concerning mutual recognition and respect provides the basis for a genuine plurality of identity and relationship practices. Within such a schema, it is possible to conceive of a spectrum at one end of which sits some form of an ethic of radical indi-vidualism. While a commitment to diversity and plurality would seem to require the inclusion of at least aspects of disenfranchised truths, this is not always the case. Oppositional discourses by their very nature are vulnerable to developing totalizing critiques. This is probably a necessary initial stage in any effort to interrupt taken-for-granted social realities. Once the critical force of such discourses gains recognition, however, a more nuanced analysis of the orthodoxies under critique may be appropriate. Such a notion is echoed in some feminist calls for research into similarities in the history of men's and women's experiences alongside analyses of differences (see McNay, 1992, pp. 36–38; Seigfried, 1989, pp. 65–66). In relation to narrative therapy, to suggest the usefulness of exploring possible links or complementarities with other approaches does not imply the need to retract original points of departure.[1] It is rather a claim that one of the ways of continuing to develop its knowledge base may include such an exploration. This could be based on aspects of approaches reported as useful by those attending therapy thus reflecting the multiple ways individuals make meaning of their experience. Just one example might be the incorporation within narrative therapy's sociopolitical framework of some explanation of the physiological processes involved in panic or anxiety attacks. This could provide people with an important acknowledgement, and enhanced understanding, of the physical dimension of such attacks,[2] while at the same time undermining the conventional separation between mind and body.

A related problem for oppositional discourses is how to stay open to critique from within. In the case of narrative therapy, an appreciation by adherents of its preparedness to address the ways in which therapies are implicated in reproducing social control – for instance in relation to homophobia, sexism, racism, classism – may give rise to a reluctance to criticize other aspects of the approach. Moreover, criticism from adherents of privileged conventional approaches can generate a united front among those adopting a more radical, less mainstream perspective. Given the potential for these and other factors to inhibit internal critique, and in keeping with the Foucauldian spirit of narrative therapy, it may be useful to foreground Foucault's warning that "everything is dangerous", thus requiring ongoing reassessment of what constitutes "the main danger" (Rabinow, 1984, p. 343). While the influence of therapeutic orthodoxies remains substantial and from the narrative therapy perspective requires ongoing challenge, its own increasing influence is likely to generate additional dangers. As Robert Doan argues, no theory or practice regardless of its intentions to redress issues of injustice can put itself beyond the danger of becoming the new orthodoxy or the final word on a domain of human experience. Confronting this type of danger would be in keeping with the values underpinning narrative therapy. Thus Doan claims that one would expect a therapy which problematizes discourses adopting a normative standard against which individuals are evaluated and judged to be deficient, to welcome individual creativity and diversity within its own ranks, and to resist perceiving itself as privileged in relation to all other approaches (Doan, 1998, pp. 380–382). Similarly, Bird points to the contradiction between any notion of a narrative therapy *model* and many of the assumptions informing therapists' engagement with narrative ideas and practices (Bird, 2000, p. ix).

Maintaining an openness to critique also can be facilitated through an emphasis on reflexivity. Such a notion is suggested in White's claim that other therapists' interest in this approach lies precisely in its articulation of, and the potential for extending, their own preferred values and practices. Emphasizing the reflexive dimension of engaging with narrative ideas and practices helps avoid the danger of attributing too much autonomy to any approach or model. This is not to downplay the significance of narrative therapy's innovative contribution to the development of different practices. Rather it underlines the interactive process involved in therapists' engagement with these. For instance, for some therapists an appreciation of the compatibility of narrative therapy and aspects of feminism can provide the basis for extending both. Jean Grimshaw points to numerous feminist critiques of the conventional medical model informed by a mystique of expertise and the reduction of those seeking assistance to the status of powerless "patients". She notes that in many women's health groups knowledge sharing and encouraging participation have been a crucial form of resistance to such disempowering processes (Grimshaw, 1986, pp. 220, 222–223). Feminism's historic influence on the development of narrative therapy (discussed in Chapter 6) continues through the work of feminist practitioners in a wide range of areas – including sexual abuse, domestic violence, mental and physical health, eating problems, self-harm, heterosexism, race and culture discrimination, sexuality, mothering, heterosexual relationships and community work (see Russell and Carey, 2003, pp. 72–73).

Engagement with the ideas and practices of narrative therapy by feminists and others is likely to give rise to a multiplicity of creative approaches in a broad range of areas. For Doan, this plurality requires an acknowledgement by those within the narrative therapeutic community "that we share certain assumptions, and celebrate the different forms these assumptions can take 'in action' by various personalities" (Doan, 1998, p. 385). Moreover, the dynamic quality of therapeutic practices is important in terms of the different requirements of those seeking assistance and the concrete effects of these practices in their local communities (Freedman and Combs, 1996, p. 275). For example, this approach has been identified as compatible with indigenous culture precisely because of its potential "to evolve for Aboriginal use in consultation with Aboriginal people" (Reclaiming Our Stories . . ., 1995, p. 20). The lack of conformity to a uniform mode of practice enhances the possibility of constructive debate within a broad community of practitioners influenced by narrative and social constructionist ideas. It encourages ongoing assessment of how adequately a theoretical description represents actual experience within the therapeutic relationship (Bird, 2000, p. xix). In this regard, simply locating differences in the personalities of therapists, as Doan suggests, diminishes the extent to which certain forms of practice may reflect a further development of the ideas. It is to this type of debate that I now turn.

THE MISSING HEART

Mary Wylie describes the impact of White's work as deriving not simply from the introduction of new techniques developed from an interesting theoretical framework, but from "something like what 18th-century English evangelist John Wesley called 'the heart strangely warmed'" (Wylie, 1994, p. 47). Perhaps it is something akin to this quality that Bruce Hart finds missing from the dominant account of White's practice. In describing White's work, he points to his ability "to engage children and parents in humorous and playful interventions" (Hart, 1995, p. 186) and his very respectful ways of connecting with, and positioning himself in relation to, individuals and families. While these more intangible aspects are harder to articulate, they nonetheless may be crucial in both the success of the therapeutic work itself and its appeal to other therapists. In some written accounts of the work which present verbatim transcripts of therapeutic conversations, the qualities of respect and connection are quite palpable and contribute significantly to what makes them so emotionally moving. This raises the question of why these aspects are not given more emphasis in the literature. Perhaps it is assumed that this way of working automatically encourages a stance of respect and connection on the part of therapists. It also may be, as Bird suggests, that such factors are less easy to articulate than more concrete frameworks and techniques precisely because they have been placed beyond accepted standards for academic publication. Pointing to the possible gender implications informing such standards, she poses the question of whether an absence of emphasis in therapeutic literature and therapist training generally on emotion-related qualities might be due to the perception of them as encompassing women's work (Bird, 1993, p. 83). In her own engagement with narrative and other ideas, she explicitly refers to the therapeutic conversation as "extremely evocative of emotions" and its style as something that is experienced or felt as opposed to heard. She emphasizes moreover the importance of "*a feeling for words*" in order to develop questions which explore the subtlety and varying shades of meaning ascribed to everyday language. She further points to the need to listen not only to ideas but also to the body and to and for the emotions in order to "access a richer tapestry of potential meanings" (Bird, 2000, p. 18). In her experience, this increases the possibility of "a meeting of words that touch the heart" (2000, p. 18). In turn, this crosses the experiential divide and creates an environment in which "we sit together, stripped bare of pretence, facing our humanity in all its fragility and magnificence" (2000, p. 18). She depicts the investigation and articulation of the language of feelings as the inevitable outcome of a full engagement with the complexity of people's lives (2000, pp. 8, 16, 20).

THE REPRODUCTION OF DOMINANT LANGUAGE PRACTICES

A further strand of critique focuses on gendered language practices. Heather Elliott raises the question of whether the radical force of narrative therapeutic "counter-practices" is undercut by the use of dominatory language:

> Narrative therapy is, like our language generally, filled with warring metaphors. For example, take phrases such as "taking a stand against [the problem]", "standing up to [the problem]", "conquering", "battling with". Although we reason that we are turning the language of oppression around to work against the problem, we still perpetuate a patriarchal language of domination . . . Do we really want to do this? I think, as therapists, we need to be ever cognizant and vigilant about preserving the very thing that we are working to transform. This is not to say that we can never use certain metaphors. But perhaps we can attempt to find and use metaphors from other landscapes within our work.
>
> (Elliott, 1998, p. 55)

A similar concern is expressed by Kathleen Stacey about the common privileging of dominant definitions of the protest/resistance metaphor in the work of many therapists influenced by narrative ideas. She sees this as reflecting an association with commonly held political notions of resistance as active defiance. The usefulness of such a definition in many situations is acknowledged, particularly those that are life-threatening or born from histories of oppression, or in which eliminating the problem is possible. Nonetheless, she points to the way in which its privileging overshadows alternative understandings of protest and resistance that may be more appropriate in other circumstances, for instance when it is not possible to eliminate the problem, such as in the case of chronic health problems or learning difficulties. In these situations finding ways to live in some kind of harmony or compromise with problems is likely to be more useful than notions of beating or conquering them (Stacey, 1997, *passim*). Moreover, even when problems appear to be beatable, dominant notions of resistance may be inappropriate. Jill Freedman gives the example of working with a family in which the partner/father Glenn had a long history of struggle with depression. When she realized there were some depression-free times, Freedman initially assumed this would be useful to explore and possibly build on. Responding to the family's reluctance to pursue this, however, she discovered that experience had taught them it was better to develop a different sort of relationship with depression rather than aiming to eliminate it altogether. Because the latter had proved fruitless in the past, the family had developed instead a relationship of co-existence with Glenn's depression which relegated it to a certain low-level, manageable position (Freedman and Combs, 1996, pp. 129–130). Stacey claims that while alternative notions of protest and resistance *are* used in narratively informed approaches, these tend to be understated (Stacey, 1997, pp. 30, 42–47).

A further reproduction of commonly accepted language practices is reflected in a tendency towards dichotomous thinking. For instance, in Leela Anderson's view, one of the shortcomings of narrative therapy's emphasis on the central metaphors of dominant and alternative stories is that this can lead to problematic and preferred experience being construed in oppositional terms. She gives the example of the common dichotomy between feelings of despair and hope. The problem with this type of thinking is that it tends to posit hope as a static, all or nothing kind of quality or experience. If the therapeutic goal of working with despair is connected automatically to this type of hope experience, its absence can render people vulnerable to an exacerbation of despair with serious implications for their well-being. Rather than encouraging the use of commonly accepted binaries, therefore, she sees it as more helpful to explore with people what the reduction of despair might mean and how this might be named, including exploration of what facilitates movement towards or away from the preferred state (Anderson, personal communication, October 2000).

For Bird, moving beyond binary notions importantly acknowledges the complex and contradictory relationship to personal attributes often held by those who have been subject to the trauma of physical, emotional or sexual abuse (Bird, 2000, p. 177). Thus in relation to, say, hope it allows for the possibility of a multiplicity of engagements including, for example, "limited hope", "protective hope", "hope with safety", "pretend hope", "wait and see hope" (Bird, 2000, p. 180). A further example can be seen in relation to an attribute such as courage. While for many survivors of abuse acknowledgement of courage or resistance as all-encompassing notions is unlikely, they may be able to recognize a certain *degree of* courage or *a sense of* resistance in relation to the abuse and its effects. In this way "[t]he movement away from binaries provides conditions for a rich and multidimensional exploration . . . to expose the [intricate] influences that are shaping [of people's] relationship with the self and with life" (Bird, 2000, p. xiv). It also assists people to move away from an entrapment in polarizing language practices – for example, "I never belonged", "I can't forgive" – which can invoke a range of disempowering feelings. Experimenting with linguistic practices beyond polarities enables development of what Bird calls "language for the in-between", for instance a notion of "adequate belonging" or "partial forgiveness". This type of language increases the potential for articulating and performing a more diverse and nuanced range of experience, and undermines belief in the solidity of commonly understood notions of pathology and normality. In contrast to polarizing language practices, language for the in-between implies the possibility of activity, movement and context (Bird, 2000, pp. 13, 14, 21, 23–24).

EMPHASIZING THE RELATIONAL

The above type of critique underlines the broader issue of whether the reproduction of conventional language forms may be perpetuating modes of social practice which narrative therapy professes to challenge. In Bird's view, this is the case in relation to its key strategy of externalization which emphasizes the idea of the problem as separate from the person. She sees this type of oppositional structure as linguistically reinforcing the dominant cultural belief in the self as autonomous and self-regulating. This undercuts the commitment to a notion of identity as always constituted in relation to specific sociohistorical ideas and practices (Bird, 2000, pp. x, 7–9, 47). This type of concern parallels one of the criticisms levelled at Foucault's later work. In relation to his treatment of others, Lois McNay depicts his notion of the self which remains within a subject–object dynamic as reflecting a failure to free his thought from a conventional atomized notion of subjectivity (McNay, 1992, pp. 171, 174–175). In the therapeutic context, rather than encouraging a person to define her or his self in opposition to the problem, Bird emphasizes the relational connection between the person and the problem. Building on the idea of externalization, she posits an alternative notion of "relational externalizing". This generates a shift from the idea of an individual self to the notion of a self always in relationship. Thus rather than simply externalizing the problem of, say, fear in order to generate a sense of distance or space between a person and the problem, a person's relationship to fear would be explored. This can include looking at the ideas and practices of fear "in relationship to people's . . . lives, in relationship to the past, present, future, in relationship to others, and in relationship to prevailing cultural ideas" (Bird, 2000, p. 8).

As the latter suggests, emphasizing a self in relationship facilitates exploration of the historical, cultural and gender dimensions of problems or concerns. This type of contextualizing enquiry enables people to reflect on their self-interpretations and experiences in relation to culturally available ideas for meaning-making. In this way the relationship between power relations and commonly accepted ways of thinking and acting can be explored, enabling people to connect with ideas beyond pathologizing notions of the self. Implicit in the language used in this type of conversation is the idea that the problem identified by a person does not capture the totality of who they are. It also implies that the self is not "the sole regulator of life events and the meanings attributed to these . . . events" (Bird, 2000, p. 8). From Bird's perspective, the conceptual space created between the person and their concern is not a separation but rather an emphasis on the relational. This generates a linguistic shift which profoundly alters the way people engage with the self. She sees relational externalizing as providing a way of *performing*, as opposed to simply valuing, the idea of a self always in relationship to a set of historically specific cultural ideas and practices (Bird, 2000, pp. x–xi, 7–9, 15, 20, 65, 89, 128–129).

The relational externalizing conversation continues to be used in the exploration of experience that stands outside impoverishing self-description. In this way, attributes or ways of being identified by people as preferred are not seen as intrinsic to them but rather the self is conceived of as constituted by ideas and practices which can be engaged with actively in an ongoing manner. This means that when people feel less connected to preferred ways of being they are less likely to pathologize themselves. This, in turn, clears a space for considering what supports connection and disconnection to these attributes or states (Bird, 2000, pp. xi, 47, 82, 128).

Bird does not position her work within narrative therapy. She does, however, credit Michael White's early work on externalizing questions and those exploring the relative impact of problems and acts of resistance as an important influence. She also points to a shared "passionate engagement with issues of justice and ethics" with those who describe themselves as narrative therapists (Bird, 2000, pp. ix, 89). At the same time, her work reflects a more thoroughgoing emphasis on the linguistic basis of the understandings people hold about themselves and their life experience. In this regard, it appears closer to many of the critical approaches that have developed within the discipline of psychology.[3] Overall Bird draws on an eclectic range of sources. Perhaps it is a combination of the distance from, and the proximity to, narrative therapy which results in her incisive critique. Given the extent to which we all are enmeshed in dominant identity conceptions regardless of intellectual commitments to the contrary, the development of language practices capable of actively disturbing notions of self-contained individuality is important. In this way, just as narrative therapy's focus on the positive dimension of our relations with others and on gender relations enables a more effective operationalization of Foucault's thought (as elaborated in Chapter 6), Bird's critique does likewise in relation to narrative practices of externalization.

FEMINISM AND THE RELATIONAL

Before looking at the implications of "relational externalizing" for self-policing, it may be useful to examine the relationship between this approach and certain other therapies which emphasize relationality. One important influence on such therapies has been feminist object relations theory, whose deconstruction of the gender biases of psychoanalytic theory has made aspects of this approach more amenable to feminist thought (Seu and Heenan, 1998, p. 223). This is reflected in the influential work of Luise Eichenbaum and Susie Orbach which focuses on the dynamics of the mother/daughter relationship in contemporary western societies. These societies typically are characterized by exclusive early female mothering in an environment which devalues the idea of women as persons in their own right. In such a context, Eichenbaum and Orbach describe a cycle in which mothers, themselves emotionally malnourished, consciously and uncon-sciously transmit to their daughters the importance of curtailing their own emotional needs and of defining themselves in relation to the ability to nurture others. This results in inadequately nurtured daughters who are unable to sufficiently separate from their mothers, leading to a poorly developed sense of self and the likelihood of adult relationship difficulties. The existence of such a cycle is seen to shed light on many women's continued participation in, and replication of, patriarchal norms. The impact of exclusive early female mothering on boys is conceived as differ-ently problematic. While dominant social prescriptions for male identity encourage successful separation from the mother, this is achieved through boys defining themselves in opposition to her. The resultant underdevel-opment of relational capacities makes it difficult for males to meet women's emotional needs. This is so despite the fact that their own ability to be relatively autonomous is created and sustained through women's unacknowledged nurturance. In this account, part of the solution entails therapeutic work with women to redress repressed needs and desires derived from the experience of inadequate early nurturing. Through such a process, first with the "mother" therapist and then with others, a woman is able to develop a stronger sense of self, both connected to and separate from others (Eichenbaum and Orbach, 1985). In a later work, Orbach and Eichenbaum claim that the developing subjectivity of a woman within the therapeutic environment also requires the presence of the therapist as a whole subject. This necessitates inclusion of the countertransference experience for analysis and understanding. In this way, the likelihood of therapist complicity in the re-enactment of a woman's habitual relational dynamics is diminished and the opportunity provided for her to engage with another subject (Orbach and Eichenbaum, 1993).

The link between identity and connection with others is central to another form of therapy based on a relational model of women's development. This approach points to, and seeks to revalue, women's capacity to form mutually empathic, empowering, interdependent relationships. Beginning in the mother/daughter relationship, this capacity is depicted in terms of ongoing engagement in increasingly more complex and flexible relational interactions which provide the context for other aspects of development, including creativity, competence, initiative, agency, self-reliance, and so forth. In this way, connectedness with others is seen as central to the emergence of an individual sense of self and as an ongoing aspect of female identity. The problem is that women's relational capacities are socially devalued through the elevation of a more self-contained notion of identity associated with masculinity. It is argued, moreover, that the common underdevelopment of relational capacities in males frequently frustrates women's attempts to engage in mutually empathic relationships with men, for which they tend to blame themselves. From the perspective of this framework, therapy provides a forum for the validation of women's relational selves and the development of greater self-empathy. It also enables validation of the tensions generated by living within a social environment in which the value of emotional responsiveness and inter-personal sensitivity is denied in relation to a wide range of life activities (Jordan et al., 1991).[4]

From the above-sketched outlines, several differences between these types of therapies and the relational externalizing approach are evident. While all three perspectives seek to challenge disabling intra- and inter-personal effects of gender power relations and emphasize the importance of the therapeutic relationship itself, Eichenbaum and Orbach's approach focuses on unconscious processes deriving from the mother/daughter relationship and personal change is facilitated through the provision of adequate mothering. Conversely, the relational development approach focuses on the growth-promoting dynamics of the mother/daughter relationship and change is seen to lie in a validation of women's relational capacities and the development of a more empathic connection with the self. In relational externalizing conversations, the shape and content of explorations of the past are not predetermined but rather emerge out of the therapeutic enquiry. The mother/daughter relationship is not a particular feature of the approach and the focus on relational identity extends beyond a connection with important others to include the various cultural ideas and practices which shape self and life understandings. This leads to an emphasis on the importance of negotiating an understanding of the language informing the meaning people make of their experience and the development of linguistic practices which facilitate a relational engagement with frameworks of meaning. This type of engagement helps counter the reduction of people's experience to static internalized states, thereby allowing the negotiation of other possible understandings of the self and life events. In relation to the issue of difference, Bird's emphasis on the importance of exploring the various contexts in which people's self-descriptions develop and are reinforced seems better able to address the multiplicity of ways in which women's selves are constructed through a range of social relations, including race, class, sexuality and health.

RELATIONAL EXTERNALIZING AND SELF-POLICING

It is the focus on generating *an experience of* relationality which renders Bird's critique of narrative externalization practices useful in explorations of self-policing. I noted earlier the subversive potential of undermining the idea that negative self-policing practices form an inevitable part of psychic make up. Given the powerful hold and disempowering effects of such an idea, the importance of finding ways to facilitate an active relationship with self-policing practices cannot be overestimated. Using Bird's approach, this could involve investigating the ideas and practices of self-policing – for example *the* self-surveillance, *the* self-criticism, *the* self-recriminations, *the* unfavourable comparisons with others, *the* isolation (or whatever is deemed the best description of negative self-practices) – *in relation to* a woman's sense of self, her relationships with others and her life generally in the past, present and possible future. Thus if a woman identifies a self-critical attitude, she can be asked how *it* has her thinking and feeling about, and acting towards, herself; how *it* affects her experience of intimate relations, her parenting, her friendships; whether *it* intrudes into her work or study; how *it* has her viewing the past; what possibilities *it* presents her with for the future, and so on. This is not to suggest bombarding a woman with these types of questions one after another. Each question will emit responses that provide potentially rich avenues for further exploration of both the effects of self-policing (not all of which may be experienced negatively) and the tactics of power and control which support and reinforce it. Following Bird, the effectiveness of this process can be optimized by attending carefully to the language people use to describe their lived experience in order to negotiate a shared meaning. In this way, women are supported to reflect on, try out and claim the language that best describes their experience.

Out of this exploration, a clearer picture will emerge of the extent and intensity of self-policing practices and the type of feelings, attitudes and practices they incite and rely on. While continuing to use non-internalizing language, the history of a woman's relationship to self-policing can be researched to identify who and what has supported and reinforced it. This can be assisted by questions which help to contextualize such support, including exploring any ideas and practices in a woman's family, social network, workplace and/or the broader society which tend to reinforce the self-policing. Reflection also can be encouraged on who such ideas and practices benefit and who they work against. As Bird notes, this type of enquiry brings into focus the community within which individuals and their families are immersed. Exposing the relationship between individual struggle and commonly accepted ideas and practices enhances possibilities for moving beyond a static, pathologizing self-description (Bird, 2000, pp. 8, 65, 74). In this way, women can begin to gain a clearer sense of the cultural structures of inequity relating to gender, race, class, sexuality, health, and so forth that have provided the context for many of their struggles in life. In this process immobilizing feelings of self-blame are diminished and space is created for thinking about ways of actively intervening in the relationship with self-policing.

In revising the relationship with self-policing, the relational aspects of preferred ways of relating to the self continue to be emphasized. This offers an important counter to any habituated tendency on the part of the therapist or client to locate preferred states and attitudes within natural or essential characteristics. Rather women can work towards strengthening their relationship with attributes such as confidence, trust, hope, acceptance, playfulness, spontaneity, and so forth. In this way, the active participation (agency) required to bring these into their lives is not diminished (Stacey, 1997, p. 36). Emphasizing one's relationship to preferred practices also lessens the power of self-policing when such practices are less present in people's lives. Thus a focus on one's relationship to, say, confidence at such times is more enabling than the idea of one no longer being a confident person. Rather than construing confidence as a static internalized state, this acknowledges the reality that both preferred attributes (such as confidence or trust)[5] and unwanted ones (such as debilitating forms of self-criticism or self-doubt) ebb and flow in line with personal circumstance and social context. For instance, it is hardly surprising that one's relationship to self-confidence is likely to wane in an unsupportive or devaluing environment or conversely that it will be nurtured in a supportive milieu. A relational focus encourages reflection on the context within which preferred attributes tend to be more present or absent. As Bird contends, this precludes any attribute acquiring a neutral status, highlighting instead the notion that all attributes, all ideas, are sustained by forces greater than "I" (Bird, 2000, pp. 7–8, 20, 47). A focus on the relationship with attributes moreover allows for the possibility of *degrees and varying types of*, say, confidence or trust or self-doubt. This challenges a common cultural tendency to think in terms of absolutes whereby one is either confident or not confident, trusting or unable to trust, and thus is better able to capture and validate the nuance and complexity of much lived experience. Bird's earlier mentioned emphasis on developing "language for the in-between" is significant in this regard.

As noted in Chapter 3, the process of actively intervening in the relationship with self-policing can be aided by exploring instances of resistance. As bell hooks argues, acknowledging such resistance does not necessitate turning a blind eye to acts of victimization but is rather the recognition of a capacity for agency (hooks, 1996, pp. 58, 61). Foregrounding often forgotten or obscured histories of resistance undermines the power of impoverishing self-understandings and helps strengthen belief in one's ability to think, act and feel differently in the present and future. It also helps clarify women's preferred self-attitudes and understandings and the values informing these. Keeping in mind that what counts as an act of resistance ultimately can be determined only by those attending therapy, it also can be helpful to identify, and strengthen links to, histories of resistance by various family members or others across generations – for example a woman may connect with personal qualities or events in her mother's, aunt's and/or grandmother's life (or that of male family members) which challenge patriarchal norms. This type of "re-membering" process provides an audience of support and legitimation for revised relations with the self. Other forms of audience also can be enlisted for this purpose. Finally, charting histories of resistance enables a realization of the feminist project, at an individual level, of rediscovering and revaluing women's experiences (McNay, 1992, p. 12). It, moreover, reflects the idea that individuals are simultaneously produced by and resist patriarchal power, thereby cutting across any idea of women as passive receptors of such power.[6]

GLIMPSES OF FREEDOM

It is difficult to convey the sense of empowerment expressed by women when, against years of training and habit, the shackles of self-policing begin to loosen. While not wanting to downplay the frequent complexity and ongoing nature of this process, it entails a growing sense of acceptance, belief, appreciation and love of the self – qualities difficult to achieve within patriarchal prescriptions for feminine identity. Thus a student concerned about her performance may find herself checking out the experiences of peers instead of automatically pathologizing and isolating herself. When an individual realizes she is not alone in struggling with a particular problem she gets a glimpse, often for the first time, that issues beyond personal culpability might be afoot. In another example, a young woman whose life has been dominated by anorexia nervosa may begin to hear herself say "nobody's perfect" rather than automatically subjecting herself to gruelling physical and emotional punishments for failing to meet its perfectionist demands. A mother may find herself noticing positive aspects of her parenting. A survivor of child sexual abuse may begin to experience a move towards self-belief or self-love. These are powerful experiential moments of resistance to oppressive practices of power which give rise to the possibility of preferred constructions of self and relationship with profound consequences for enhanced quality of life.

NON-ESSENTIALIST IDENTITY

The significance of such transformative moments lies in their demonstration that taken-for-granted, seemingly fixed notions of identity are an illusion. Once this has been experienced a more fluid notion of identity becomes possible. Discovering that aspects of the self can be superseded through active intervention in one's own life gives rise to the possibility of ongoing destabilization of fixed categories of identity. This is not, therefore, an argument for advancing any particular notion of what it means to be a woman, or indeed the idea that there is any natural or inevitable female identity. Such an argument would involve substituting one set of privileged ideas with another as opposed to facilitating resistance to the defining power of privileged knowledges (Law and Madigan, 1994, p. 5). As Vanessa Swan argues, the challenge for a progressive feminist therapy is how to open up space

> for dialogue and the local contestation of knowledge, as opposed to the universal or commonsensical construction of knowledge. It is not about defining singular, better and healthier ways of being . . . [as much as] problematizing the universal and privileged nature of some knowledges. It is their privileged position after all – their common sense – which makes them implements of exclusion and oppression.
>
> (Swan, 1999, p. 106)

As suggested, the creation of a space in which the privileging of certain ideas and practices can be questioned opens up possibilities for personal agency that are precluded when identity categories are seen as fixed or foundational. In this way a range of different gender styles and identities can be fostered. Such an orientation implicitly challenges what Judith Butler has called "the regulatory fiction of heterosexual coherence" (Butler, 1990b, p. 338) which stabilizes and unifies the category of woman (1990b, pp. 338–339). Butler points out that gender prescriptions require continual performance, which means that ones other than those which have taken on the appearance of the natural are possible (Butler, 1990a, pp. 141, 145–146, 148). In this light the task is "to redescribe those possibilities that *already* exist, but which exist within cultural domains designated as culturally unintelligible and impossible" (1990a, pp. 148–149) – for example, the forging and celebration of a range of non-heterosexual identities and communities.

Finally, while advocating the merits of non-essentialism, this approach reflects a relationship to ethics based on empirical knowledge of the impoverishing effects of oppression and marginalization. It is precisely this type of knowledge which precludes any encouragement of self-understandings involving the exploitation, domination or abuse of others.

THE TENACITY OF SELF-POLICING

Having spoken about the power of transformative moments[7] in which women begin to alter their relationship with disabling practices of the self, it is important not to underestimate the entrenched position of self-policing. One problem that can arise is "backlash". This can be understood as a sudden reappearance, often in intense form, of the very negative thoughts and feelings from which one is attempting to gain distance. Backlash often occurs following a person's move away from the influence of disabling thoughts and feelings. Its intensity can be both frightening and demoralizing, often convincing individuals they were mistaken to believe in their efforts to transform negative identity practices. It is as though the understandings which hitherto have played a dominant role in a person's relationship with the self suddenly spring back with renewed vigour to undermine the challenge to their position. Like many habituated practices they are unlikely to disappear quietly or quickly. A useful response to backlash experiences is the cultivation of an active strategy of observing their tactics and recognizing the way they try to undermine any attempt to perform alternative self-understandings. This type of non-confrontational strategy corresponds with a commonly expressed desire by women to move beyond a psychic state characterized by "internal battle". Moreover, alerting individuals to the possibility of backlash on the basis of other people's experience can break down a sense of isolation and individual failure. It is also important to explore the context in which backlash is more likely to survive. For example, a supportive environment by family/friends/workplace/social institutions may diminish the likelihood of its appearance or the intensity of its power. Conversely, an unsupportive environment may enhance these. Central to the disempowering of backlash seems to be an experiential sense that negative self-understandings, regardless of their compelling nature, do not speak the truth about oneself.

A further problem that may be encountered when women embark on the journey towards preferred identity practices is the resurgence of self-policing in the service of newly incorporated ideas and practices. Thus women can find themselves rigorously evaluating their ability to maintain new self-understandings. Indeed self-policing can intensify when women give voice to preferred identities, as failure to perform these can be interpreted as evidence of inability to change. As indicated, externalizing the relationship with preferred attributes or states offers a way of counter-ing the idea of essential qualities which one either does or does not possess. In this process, the ongoing influence of self-policing can be rendered transparent and steps taken to undermine it. For instance, if women begin to interpret intermittent slippages back to unwanted ways of being as part of the usual process of change rather than as evidence of regression, it is more difficult for disabling practices to prosper. This process can be facilitated by rendering visible any difference between a woman's response to herself and to others in a similar situation. Almost invariably when asked how she would react to such slippages in a friend's life, a woman's response is phrased in terms of encouragement and support for what would be expected setbacks from time to time in any effort to change habituated ways of thinking, feeling or acting. Moreover, women tend automatically to take into account the context in which other women's experiences take place – for example: *given what she's up against, I think she's doing really well.* The existence of one set of rules for others and another, less generous, set for the self is a common consequence of the imbalance in many women's training between other- and self-oriented care.[8] Illuminating this disparity provides a yardstick by which women can begin to move towards a relationship with the self that embodies the level of care and compassion so often extended to others. Such a notion points to the potential of the idea of friendship with the self as an antidote to self-policing. This idea is elaborated in the following chapter.

SUMMARY

This chapter looked at several strands of immanent critique of narrative therapy. In relation to the seeming paradox between a challenge to dominant notions of individualism and assisting people to develop greater personal freedom, I argued that it is the truth status of privileged under-standings of individualism that narrative therapy opposes rather than the idea of personal autonomy per se. This led into a discussion about the types of problems faced by oppositional discourses in remaining open to critique and possible ways of countering these. Another strand of critique issues a reminder of the need to avoid replicating problematic gender and language practices. Particular attention was paid to Bird's concern that narrative practices of externalization reveal the extent to which a self-regulated notion of the self is reinforced linguistically. She posits an alternative notion of "relational externalizing" as a more effective mechanism for *performing*, rather than simply valuing, a self always in relationship to a culture's ideas, practices, time and context. The incorporation of this critique promises to be useful in efforts to destabilize a common belief in the intrinsic nature of self-policing. This enhances possibilities for negotiating a different type of relationship with the self. Just as relations characteristic of self-policing and the identities it maintains are exposed as one possible set of cultural constructions, preferred practices of the self also are depicted as non-essential. This enables a sense of agency in the enactment of such practices and diminishes the potential for pathologizing oneself when they are underperformed. The process of negotiating different self-understandings is facilitated by reflecting on the context in which these are likely to prosper and by exploring histories of resistance to unwanted practices. Preferred ways of relating to and understanding the self can be enriched and strengthened through a supportive connection with others. Finally, I looked at some common problems which may be experienced when women embark on the process of change, and signalled the subversive potential of friendship with the self.

Given the power of self-policing to dominate intra-subjective relations and maintain prescribed identities, the type of self-making advocated here can be seen as an important part of women's struggle towards self-understandings over which they have a greater say. As noted earlier, disempowering ways of relating to and interpreting the self can remain intact despite the achievement of institutional and attitudinal change. This is not to downplay the need for such change. Political action to alter oppressive laws, institutions, social practices and attitudes is vital for the building of a better, fairer world. At the same time, simultaneous efforts to disturb given power relations at the intra-subjective level also contribute to the dismantling of oppressive structures. In a therapeutic environment in which women begin to gain a clearer sense of the cultural context framing many of their struggles, a sense of self-blame or personal deficiency begins to diminish. This creates space for the development of preferred self and life understandings. Moreover, when this occurs women begin to position themselves differently in the world – in their relationships with male partners/relatives/bosses, children, other women and societal expectations – albeit in the face of continuing external constraints. It is through this type of negotiation with given power relations that the status quo is disturbed at individual and local levels. Chapter 6 refers to this process in relation to the restructuring of families as a consequence of the impact of feminist ideas on women's daily lives. These types of change complement and supplement equally important institutional and structural change. Moreover, for some women change at the personal level leads to engagement in broader political action. In this regard Chapter 6 describes the activism of one group in the field of mental health.[9] Some women who undertake one-to-one therapy also become more politically active. This can include membership of committees or boards concerned with issues of which they have direct experience – for example domestic violence, child sexual assault, eating disorders, and so on – participating in demonstrations and lobbying government. While the step from micro- to broader level political action is not inevitable, for many women it becomes more likely following politicization at the personal level. In this process, women come to appreciate the extent to which dominant cultural ideas and practices have contributed to their own and others' struggles and encouraged the decontextualization of their lives.

The type of work on the self I have described would seem to correspond with McNay's emphasis on the importance of a feminist politics grounded in the "idea of woman as an active social agent capable of instituting radical change at the micro-political level" (McNay, 1992, p. 115). In thinking about the further facilitation of this type of self-making, the next chapter looks at the idea of greater care for the self.

5

AN ETHICS OF CARE FOR
THE SELF

INTRODUCTION

This chapter builds on the previous discussion by exploring the idea of
greater care for the self as a further antidote to self-policing. Drawing on
aspects of Foucault's later work, it is argued that his emphasis on the
ethical relationship one has with oneself provides a useful framework for
the notion of enhanced care. Within such a framework, care for the self
entails an ethos of ongoing critique and transformation of the discursive
practices that shape identity. In thinking about the operationalization of
this type of care, I suggest the value of friendship as an organizing principle
in relations with the self. The idea of women's friendship with the self,
however, highlights certain limitations of the Greek-inspired notion of care
for the self that informs Foucault's work on ethics. The notions of
conquest, hierarchy, battle and domination around which ancient relations
with the self are structured appear closer to the strict overseer type of intra-
subjective relation characteristic of self-policing. Yet this is precisely the
type of stance towards the self that needs to be overcome or at least
reduced. In thinking about an orientation more likely to undermine self-
policing and facilitate the type of creative self-making advocated by
Foucault, I point to the work of bell hooks and Maria Lugones. A fuller
discussion of different attitudes to the self is articulated in the section on
friendship with the self.

Prior to this, Lois McNay's concern about the primacy Foucault
attributes to care of the self is discussed. I also build on her criticism of a
traditional mind/body split in Foucault's work on self-fashioning. This
refers to the way in which the conventional practice of privileging the
rational can encourage a sense of failure when women underperform
preferred identity practices. Finally, I signal the need for a more holistic
conception of care characterized by the indissociability of giving and
receiving.

AN ETHICS OF CARE FOR THE SELF

In earlier chapters, I argued that Foucault's depiction of the key role of self-policing in maintaining dominant identity practices illuminates an important aspect of women's struggle towards greater self-definition. Interestingly, this insight into the modern system of social control seems to be absent from his later work on ethics. This may be due, in part, to a continued inattention to issues of gender. McNay has pointed to Foucault's blurring of distinctions between those practices of the self that are more readily accessible to self-fashioning and those which are less so because of their deep inscription on the body and psyche, for example those relating to gender and sexuality (McNay, 1994, p. 155). Despite these lacunae, some aspects of his later work may provide a useful framework for countering self-policing practices and the given identities they support. In his work on ethics, Foucault singles out the relation to the self as a discrete component of morality:

> there is another side to the moral prescriptions, which most of the time is not isolated as such but is, I think, very important: the kind of relationship you ought to have with yourself, *rapport à soi*, which I call ethics, and which determines how the individual is supposed to constitute himself as a moral subject of his own actions.
>
> (Rabinow, 1984, p. 352)

The significance for women of Foucault's emphasis on the intra-subjective relationship lies in its implicit challenge to the dichotomizing of self- and other-directed care. As noted in Chapter 2, in women's general training the establishment of ethical relations with others frequently has entailed forsaking oneself as a person deserving equal consideration. Conversely in Foucault's account of antiquity, relations of integrity with others require active participation in the fashioning of one's own ethical identity. This involves practices of care for the self through which individuals (free men) are able to establish a relationship of self-mastery over the passions and basic appetites. Such practices are oriented towards achieving a full enjoyment of oneself, setting an example for future generations and establishing the basis for ethical relations with others. This ethics does not take the form of a universal law but is rather a personal choice for those motivated towards an aesthetic lifestyle. It involves a particular art of life requiring the development of practical wisdom about the appropriate ways to behave in a range of circumstances (Foucault, 1986).

Foucault realizes the folly of attempting to transpose practices from the past onto a completely different set of social arrangements in the present. Nonetheless, as Jana Sawicki notes, he thinks the Greek idea of the self

83

working to improve and transform itself could apply to current endeavours to forge new modes of identity (Sawicki, 1998, p. 105). What he admires in classical ethics is the scope afforded to individual creativity in relation to general social and moral rules. He thinks this type of personal aesthetics has the potential to counter the tendencies in modern society towards sameness and bland conformity to given norms (McNay, 1992, pp. 85–86). The type of creative self-making envisaged by Foucault does not presuppose the uncovering of a natural essence (Kritzman, 1988, pp. 50–51). As noted, he sees the notion of historically contingent identity as offering greater scope for the development and expression of human creative powers. This is reflected in his advocacy of a contemporary ethos of ongoing critique and transformation of ourselves.

Such an ethos has the potential to encourage a type of attentiveness to the self so often missing from women's lives. This lack of attentiveness, rather than increasing the likelihood of women exploiting or dominating others as in Foucault's account of ancient ethics, holds the reverse danger. An absence of caring attention to the self can render women vulnerable to exploitation or abuse. It also has the potential to deprive women of satisfying relations with the self, or in ancient terms a full enjoyment of oneself. When care for others is the primary focus, knowledge about one's own desires, needs, values, tastes, beliefs, and so forth can be patchy or even non-existent. This is not surprising as women's caretaking role frequently entails a forgoing of their own knowledges in order to please and accommodate others (Dickerson *et al.*, 1994, p. 9). Conversely, when the relationship one has with oneself is conceived as an important component of ethics, a space is created for the generation of one's own knowledges and skills. This involves creative interaction with given identity practices, standards and norms through which a reshaping of one's relationship with the self, others and life begins to take form. As in Foucault's work, this does not entail the discovery of intrinsic qualities but is rather a remaking of the self in accordance with different women's preferred cultural ideas, values and practices including, as Judith Butler contends, those yet to be articulated (Butler, 1990a, pp. 148–149).

THE POLITICS OF SELF-MASTERY

Although Foucault's work on ethics provides useful avenues for thinking about ways in which the harmful effects of self-policing on women's sense of self can be lessened, his conception of care for the self is not without limitations. These have been usefully highlighted by Lois McNay. The following sections summarize some of McNay's concerns. They also gesture toward some alternative attitudes to the self. These are articulated more fully in the section proposing that women become friends to themselves.

While Foucault distanced himself from the sexist (and elitist) dimension of ancient ethics (Rabinow, 1984, pp. 344, 346), McNay points to his failure to critique the privileging of a masculine self in the Greek theme of self-mastery from which he derives the notion of an ethics of the self. In these practices, the "virile" nature of self-mastery involved a battle against the excessive and feminine aspects of one's character. This inferiorizing of the womanly is echoed at the social level through the performance of mastery over others. Thus despite Foucault's assertion that one cannot draw uncritically on practices from another era, McNay argues that he appears to do just that in relation to the theme of self-mastery. Moreover, she sees the notion of "virile self-mastery" as enhanced through his depiction of Charles Baudelaire the dandy as the archetypal self-inventing individual of modernity. From a feminist perspective, this is seen as problematic not simply because of the well-known misogyny characterizing Baudelaire's work but because it illuminates Foucault's relatively uncritical celebration of "a certain tradition which normalizes as *the* experience of modernity a *particular* and gendered set of practices" (McNay, 1994, p. 149). This is incompatible with his insistence on a rigorous, detailed self-critique as the initial task of an ethics of the self. McNay argues that he assumes, rather than critically investigates, the radical force of the male avant-garde tradition of literature embodied in Baudelaire's work. Moreover, he does not take into account the problem of "a contemporary morality that addresses itself to women as ethical subjects but draws, nevertheless, on a tradition in which woman has historically been positioned as the 'beautiful object'" (McNay, 1994, p. 151). Thus she claims that while Foucauldian ethics purport to begin from embedded practices, they actually ignore the possible implications of structures of gender on an aesthetics of the self (McNay, 1994, pp. 134, 149–152).[1]

McNay's critique brings to light certain similarities between the ancient practices of caring for the self favoured by Foucault and those characterizing self-policing. In Foucault's account, relations with the self in antiquity are characterized by masculine notions of control, battle, conquest and hierarchy (Foucault, 1986, pp. 66–70, 82–83, 91). This type of orientation to the self mirrors structures of domination and subordination integral to the strict overseer type of intra-subjective relationship imposed by self-policing. Thus, while Foucault's emphasis on the relationship we have with ourselves offers a useful framework for redressing the imbalance between self- and other-oriented care in many women's lives, the notion of self-mastery he draws on is unlikely to achieve this. In thinking about a more appropriate orientation to the self, bell hooks' call for relationships to be structured around the organizing principle of love suggests an alternative approach:

> Rather than organize black families around the principle of authoritarian rule of the strong over the weak, we can organize (as some of us do) our understanding of family around anti-patriarchal, anti-authoritarian models that posit love as the central guiding principle. Recognizing love as the effort we make to create a context of growth, emotional, spiritual, and intellectual, families would emphasize mutual cooperation, the value of negotiation, processing, and the sharing of resources. Embracing a feminist standpoint can serve as an inspiration for transforming the family as we now know it.
>
> (hooks, 1996, p. 73)

While hooks is referring specifically to the organization of black families in the USA, embracing such a feminist standpoint also could inspire a more enabling relationship with the self than that historically encouraged. This type of orientation encourages an exploration of the types of practices, attitudes and relationships that support love, respect and equality. In seeking to replace a patriarchal orientation to the self, women can draw on aspects of their caring relations for others. Thus an alternative to conquering, mastering or controlling unwanted thoughts, desires, feelings or acts can emerge through the reflexive application of practices associated with robust friendship. These practices include wanting the best for the other, enjoying their company, honesty, acceptance, tolerance, compassion, forgiveness, and so forth. Developing a loving attitude to the self provides a context in which the self is no longer in battle with itself and which, as hooks claims, is conducive to a flourishing of the emotions, spirit and intellect.

Maria Lugones' notion of playfulness also may be useful here. She describes playfulness as the loving attitude required for the development of non-imperialistic relations between white/Anglo women and women of colour. This type of attitude fosters the requisite willingness of white women to visit the very different worlds inhabited by other women.[2] Playfulness for Lugones involves

> openness to surprise, . . . to being a fool, . . . to self-construction or reconstruction . . . [It] is characterised by uncertainty, lack of self-importance, absence of rules or a not taking rules as sacred, a not worrying about competence and a lack of . . . resignation to a particular construction of oneself, others, and one's relation to them.
>
> (Lugones, 1990, p. 401)

She contrasts this conception of play with the agonistic notions proposed by Johan Huizinga and Hans-Georg Gadamer which ultimately involve contestation, battle, winning and losing and for which the only possible playful attitude is combative and competitive. For Lugones, such a conception of play is inimical to the development of non-imperialistic relations (Lugones, 1990, pp. 390, 393, 396, 399–400). For the present purposes, the agonistic notions of play Lugones challenges parallel the type of intra-subjective relation characteristic of self-policing. Conversely, the sense of creative curiosity, flexibility, generosity and willingness to experiment that characterizes her preferred conception of playfulness provides a way of thinking about a non-imperialistic approach to relations with the self.

The development of such an approach has the potential to generate much kinder, more flexible and enjoyable relations with the self. In turn this increases possibilities for a creative interaction with given identity practices, standards and norms through which a reshaping of self-interpretations can begin to take form. In this way, a more loving/playful orientation towards the self can play a crucial role in the type of ethics advocated by Foucault. At the same time, it provides a safeguard against care of the self turning back into another form of self-policing. Qualities of generosity, acceptance and appreciation towards the self are antithetical to the type of intra-subjective relationship required for effective self-policing.

CARE FOR OTHERS

A further concern expressed by McNay is the inadequacy of a notion of care for others in Foucault's work. Foucault claims that in ancient ethics the possibility of dominating others can only derive from a *lack of* care of one's self involving enslavement to one's desires (Foucault, 1988, p. 8). As McNay notes, however, in contemporary western societies the hierarchical structure of relations means that taking care of oneself inevitably entails attempts to dominate or silence (or perhaps just neglect) others whose inferiorization has been culturally predetermined. For instance,

> a white/male/heterosexual caring for himself correctly may necessarily imply the domination of black/female/gay "other" who, because of his/her relatively subordinate position in terms of access to resources and authority, does not have the power to resist such domination.
>
> (McNay, 1992, p. 172)

While Foucault's response may be that the white/male subject is not caring for himself properly, McNay argues that his refusal to lay down even the most general guidelines about what does and does not constitute a legitimate use of power renders his conviction about the self-limiting nature of care for the self problematic. Although he claims that a safeguard against care for the self turning into the domination of others is the co-existence of power relations and the capacity to resist them (Foucault, 1988, p. 12), in McNay's view the generalized category of resistance does not adequately take into account broad structures of inequality and discrimination which ensure that the possibilities for resistance frequently are limited for some groups. For instance, a woman's ability to leave a domestic violence situation often entails giving up a secure home and adequate income for her family (McNay, 1992, pp. 172–174).

McNay's concern makes sense against the backdrop of individualistic western cultures in which the notion of caring for the self is unlikely to incite people to investigate the ways in which their positions of privilege are maintained by the subordination of others. In this sense, against his own intention, Foucault seems to be transplanting the ancient notion of care for the self onto modern society. While in his account of ancient ethics proper care for the self ensured the non-abuse of others, care for others nonetheless remained within the constraints of strict hierarchical relations. While he clearly envisioned a modern pluralistic structure of values and identities in which the opportunity for self-experimentation is widely available (see Ransom, 1997, pp. 183–184), he does not explain how practices of care for the self will disrupt entrenched structures of domination to guarantee such an opportunity. Indeed it is possible to imagine people today practising the ancient notion of self-mastery without challenging or even recognizing the ways in which their privilege depends on the subjugation of others. This is reflected in the views of paternalistic men and white women and men who often are perplexed by accusations of sexism or racism. It also is evident in views which claim that people of colour/women/non-heterosexuals simply need to take up the equality available to all citizens and to stop complaining about marginalization. The extent to which, for example, the problem of entrenched structural racism remains invisible to those in positions of privilege is reflected in the difficulty many white people have in even acknowledging their whiteness:

> When have you heard of a white person referring to him or herself as "non-black"? We do not even think of ourselves as "white". Taking ourselves and our whiteness for granted, we do not consider our skin as a colour, we are "just people".
> (MacKinnon, 1993, p. 118)

Within the context of relations of domination and subordination, an elaboration of the notion of care for others is necessary if care for the self is to safeguard others from domination or abuse as Foucault contends.

While not wanting to downplay the importance of McNay's concerns, in light of women's practice in caring for others these may be more relevant to men than to women. The first point to make, however, is that women's caring does not necessarily include all others, not even all other women, as evidenced by histories of the relationships between black and white women, heterosexual and lesbian women and upper- and working-class women. Elizabeth Spelman argues that an emphasis on the notion of women as caring tends to obscure the often exploitative and demeaning relationships between women in positions of privilege and those deemed socially inferior (Spelman, 1991, pp. 213–214, 216–220). More generally, Joan Tronto emphasizes the conservative potential of a theory of morality built on an ethic of care. She argues that because our care for others is not distributed equally, such a morality could serve to justify caring only for those like ourselves, thereby preserving existing relationships of inequality (Tronto, 1987, pp. 659–660). Indeed, the process through which relatively privileged identities are constituted reflects white, middle-class, heterosexual women's "complicity in constructing and being constructed by the difference of the others" (Flax, 1993, p. 6). Awareness of this complicity highlights the ethical urgency of the micro- and macro-level political task of fostering a plurality of socially valued identities and modes of life.

While it is crucial to remain aware of the way in which women's traditional role as carers itself has been mediated by categories of race, class and sexuality, the general point remains that gendered processes of identity formation commonly orient women more towards the care of others (even if only select others) than of the self. Conversely such processes, again in a general sense and mediated by factors other than gender, historically have oriented men more towards an emphasis on the self, often with the expectation that others, primarily girls and women, will actively support its development and consolidation. From this perspective, it is argued that the absence in Foucault's work on ethics of an adequate way of ensuring that care for the self does not lead to the domination or abuse of others is likely to be more problematic in relation to men than it is to women. This is reflected in the greater levels of men's violence towards women, children and other men.[3] The problem for women, and some women more than others, is the expansion of other-oriented training to include those women and men socially constructed as inferior in terms of race, ethnicity, class, sexuality, and so forth. The general other-orientation of women's training could provide the groundwork for greater inclusiveness. At the same time, it is precisely an imbalance between training in care for others and care for the self which can render women vulnerable to abuse and exploitation or to a sense of identity characterized by self-doubt and self-criticism. Finding ways to assist women to increase a constructive focus on their selves is the challenge often faced by those consulted by women in the therapeutic context (see Jordan et al., 1991, p. 63). Moreover, as Sawicki notes, when women have been subject to abuse, the fragmentation of self can be such that the forms of protest individuals participate in are likely to be those that further impoverish the self, as for example in the case of self-mutilation, the misuse of alcohol/drugs or eating disorders (Sawicki, 1991, p. 106).[4] For many women, caring for the self is likely to play a crucial role in undermining and transforming disabling identity practices. This is not to understate the importance of care for others. Rather it is to underscore Foucault's point that a crucial dimension of ethical relations with others is the development of a caring relationship with the self. Because the imbalance between self- and other-care tends to work in the opposite direction in the general training of boys and men, McNay's concern about the primacy of care for the self in Foucault's work on ethics may be more relevant generally to the experience of males.

FRIENDSHIP WITH THE SELF

While women often have a sense of the potential benefits of enhanced care for the self, its unfamiliarity can give rise to feelings of selfishness in the negative sense commonly associated with this term (see Jordan *et al.*, 1991, pp. 5, 201, 283). Such feelings also can be induced or enhanced by others who are used to being the primary focus of attention in women's lives. As Jean Grimshaw notes, the common perception of women as defined by their caring role and abilities renders them particularly vulnerable and sensitive to allegations of not-caring. These may be made because women go out to work when they have small children, or because they periodically want some time away from children or elderly parents, or they say no to sex on demand from their partners. The expectation to care for others can induce feelings of guilt if women try to find some space, privacy or time for themselves (Grimshaw, 1986, p. 217). However, precisely because of women's other-oriented training, greater attention to their selves is unlikely to result in an excessive preoccupation with the self. Rather such attentiveness is aimed at redressing an imbalance between self- and other-directed care. This echoes Tronto's earlier point about moral maturity requiring a balance between care for the self and care for others. In the therapeutic context, emphasizing this notion of balance can help women resist invitations to perceive a consideration of their own needs as unduly self-centred. It is precisely the latter tendency which renders Foucault's emphasis on the fashioning of one's ethical identity useful. Alongside the notion of redressing an imbalance between self- and other-focused care, the idea that greater care for the self enhances relations of integrity with others often resonates for women. This is reflected in claims such as: "If I don't start taking care of myself, I'm not going to be much use to my children/ partner/family, etc." Even though this sort of motivation might appear suspect because it sits so comfortably within predominantly other-oriented training, it nonetheless provides a valuable entry point for enhanced relations of care for the self.

In thinking about the operationalization of greater care for the self, the idea of friendship as an organizing principle in self-relations promises to be fruitful. The notion of women's friendship with the self is emphasized by Janice Raymond. For Raymond, this type of friendship represents an act of defiance against women's training in male-defined societies to take care of the needs of others often at the cost of being absent to a knowledge and appreciation of their own needs, values, interests and beliefs. Thus she inverts the Aristotelian adage "a friend is another self" to "the Self is another friend", concluding that "[i]f, as Aristotle said, 'the friend is another self,' that Self must know its own power of being. She must be her own friend" (Raymond, 1986, p. 197). In Raymond's view, empowering friendships with others can be experienced only when women are able to value their own meanings and beliefs. This entails practices of discernment: "The habit of discernment teaches us to be loyal to our Selves, to have faith in our own insights, and to claim these as a power of scrutiny in our interactions with others" (1986, p. 173). In this way friendship with the self constitutes a crucial aspect of satisfying relations with others: "The conversation of friendship with others can be had only by those who have learned how to think with themselves, to keep themselves company" (1986, p. 222). Raymond argues that carving out a space in which women can develop friendships of integrity with their own and other selves is both a personal and political act. It is the conscious creation of a space in which patriarchal prescriptions can be destabilized and alternative identity practices explored (1986, pp. 8–10, 220–222, 230–232). This stance of enhanced self-love is not confined to women; it also has been identified as a key strategy of the black liberation struggle of the 1960s (hooks, 1996, p. 119). hooks describes love of the self as integral to those who have been subject to a dominant culture's disdain and subjugation: "Collectively, black people and our allies in struggle are empowered when we practice self-love as a revolutionary intervention that undermines practices of domination" (hooks, 1996, p. 162).

THE THERAPEUTIC CONTEXT

In the therapeutic context, one technique for developing this type of self-value is to encourage women to relate to themselves as they would to a friend.[5] This has the potential to undermine the strict overseer type of relationship characteristic of self-policing which encourages women to live according to the expectations of others. As such, it creates a space in which some of the care and compassion so often extended to others can begin to become available to the self. As suggested in the previous chapter, the notion of friendship with the self can be explored by asking women what their attitude would be towards a friend struggling with similar issues.

91

What might they say about her feelings of self-blame in relation to such issues, about the pressure she puts on herself to be a certain sort of person/ partner/mother, about her tendency to "beat herself up" for falling short of this expectation? So often women reveal qualities of acceptance, tolerance, patience, compassion and support towards others that are absent in relations with the self. This often includes a readiness to take into account various external factors contributing to the difficulties of others. When this type of orientation towards others is identified it can be useful to ask: "What would it be like to imagine extending the same level of compassion, support, tolerance, acceptance, etc. to yourself?" Even to try to imagine this can engender feelings of discomfort, so unfamiliar is such a notion to many women. A further question might be: "What difference, if any, do you think it might make to your current situation if you *were* able to be more caring and supportive towards yourself?" This type of question can assist women to gain a sense of what it might be like to become less beholden to harsh and punitive practices of the self. Reference to friendship foregrounds the possibility of an alternative orientation to the self.

Once the taken-for-granted nature of self-policing has been disturbed through an exposé of its purposes and tactics, women can begin to experiment with becoming their own friend in day to day life. This process draws again on asking a woman to imagine how she would react to a friend in the same situation as she finds herself. She can be invited to observe the type of feelings, thoughts and actions characteristic of self-policing at any given time and to consider how she might respond if this was the experience of a friend. At such times she might ask herself: "What's the difference between how I'm feeling/thinking/acting towards myself and how I would react to —— in this situation?" This type of reflection also can lead to a consideration of various personal, family and/or social contexts which may be contributing to her own problematic experience. This, in turn, can foster a more accepting attitude towards the self; for example she might find herself thinking: "Given what I'm up against (social attitudes towards single mothers or lesbian families/lack of community or family support/financial struggle, etc.), I'm actually not doing too badly as a parent."

It is not meant to imply that this type of negotiation with given power relations is easy or straightforward. The entrenched nature of such relations makes this unlikely. Moreover, to the extent that these are tied to cultural ideas and practices which support the status quo – for example to discourses about "normal" sexuality, about what it means to be a good mother, about femininity, and so forth – efforts to develop a different type of self-relationship are likely to be resisted by others. Nonetheless, the space created by undermining the idea that self-policing practices are a fixed aspect of identity, and experimentation with the alternative mode of friendship with the self can yield gradual change. Moreover, as indicated earlier, the presence of supportive others can play a significant role in the process of change. Over time, women may notice themselves resisting punitive attitudes towards the self which previously would have been automatic. An example of an account of this might go something like this:

> I was at a social event which I tend to find stressful. Usually I give myself a hard time for not saying the right thing, for talking too much or not talking enough. But on this occasion I just felt pleased that I'd gotten through something I find hard. I waited for the usual put down feelings and thoughts to come but they didn't. Instead I felt a sort of peace.

Interestingly, the greater level of self-acceptance characteristic of practices of friendship with the self does not mean that current limitations will remain. On the contrary, an acceptance of who one is in the present seems to increase possibilities for change. Conversely, when the self is in battle with itself such possibilities often diminish.

Developing qualities of friendship with the self challenges the power of self-policing to dominate intra-subjective relations and, in turn, this increases possibilities for active participation in the creative process of self-making in relation to broader questions of identity. Nonetheless, the idea of a friendly or loving orientation towards the self does not require the suppression of what are commonly thought of, particularly in relation to women, as negative emotional states – for example anger, envy, resentment, ambivalence, unhappiness. On the contrary, the cultivation of more friendly, accepting self-relations has the potential to increase recognition of, and engagement with, the multiplicity of feeling states that contribute to a full human experience. Just as the integrity of good relations with others can survive and be strengthened by periodic conflicts and differences, so too can a robust self-relationship withstand, and be enhanced by, its engagement with challenging or ambivalent emotional states.

DUALISM IN FOUCAULT'S LATER THOUGHT

Earlier, I pointed to the dualist tendency characterizing much western thought (as for example in the dichotomies posed between mind and body, reason and emotion, subject and object, etc.). I noted that this type of thinking has been a key target of feminist critique. Poststructuralists and theorists of postcolonialism also have pointed to the derogation of the "other" entailed in such thought. This kind of critique is evident in Foucault's early historical analysis. Moreover, his middle works deliberately privilege the body as a focal point for the workings of power. Nonetheless, McNay points to evidence of a traditional mind/body split in the later work on ethics. This relates to the description of self-fashioning as involving "those intentional and voluntary actions by which men not only set themselves rules of conduct, but also seek to transform themselves, to change themselves" (Foucault, 1986, p. 10). McNay points out that particularly in relation to issues of gender and sexuality, the notion of intentionality does not deal adequately with involuntary and biological dimensions of experience. She argues that, while it is crucial to keep in mind Foucault's insights into the social construction of sexuality as the most entrenched part of our selves, there are some desires and biological phenomena which a mere conscious act of self-stylization cannot overcome or alter. This is not to posit the existence of bodily impulses and desires that can never be thought about differently. Rather it is to say that altering certain aspects of sexuality requires a detailed investigation "of the network of deeply entrenched cultural norms in which our bodies are embedded" (McNay, 1992, p. 80). In McNay's view, Foucault's inability to address adequately certain elements of the fashioning of individuals as sexual subjects can be linked to his neglect of the emotional or affective dimension of sexual relations in all three volumes of *The History of Sexuality*. Although this has been ascribed to his aversion to psychoanalysis' fixation with questions of conscious and unconscious emotions, it nonetheless remains that "the notion of an aesthetics of existence is too rational or intentional a category to capture some of the affective, involuntary aspects of sexuality" (McNay, 1992, p. 80). She refers to the example of a study of adolescent working-class girls for whom getting and keeping a man generated power and status, even when this involved occupying subject positions usually considered subordinate (McNay, 1992, p. 81).

PRIVILEGING THE RATIONAL

That Foucault's later privileging of rationality is more than an unthinking adoption of conventional language practices is suggested strongly by his earlier explicit stance against dualism. Nonetheless, it does little to disturb the unrealistic expectations generated by the conventional elevation of our rational capacities. As McNay argues in relation to his work on self-fashioning, this understates the emotional and psychological dimensions of change. In (and out of) the therapeutic context, women often express frustration and a sense of failure at not being able to embody preferred identity practices. For example, a woman might say: "I know this stuff in my head, why can't I live it? I really believe this intellectually yet I keep denying it in everyday life." This dilemma can feel particularly demoralizing given the legacy of historical diminution of women's rational abilities. A woman may have a clear intellectual appreciation that she is not to blame for the abuse perpetrated on her. Yet in every fibre of her body, emotions and/or psyche she may *feel* responsible and ashamed. The dominant cultural tendency to privilege rational thinking can encourage further self-blame for her inability to embody this type of understanding. Yet given the physical and psychological nature and effects of abuse – its assault on the body, psyche, emotions and spirit – in addition to likely mental and/or emotional manipulation by the abuser, community reluctance to acknowledge abuse as a widespread social problem and the prevalence of woman-blame – it is hardly surprising that an intellectual appreciation of blamelessness will not in and of itself result in its embodiment.

Another example of the multi-dimensional nature of self-fashioning relates to gender prescriptions for women's bodies. A woman may think that certain commonly accepted uniform standards for the size, shape or look of women's bodies are oppressive but nonetheless remain captured by such prescriptions. This is hardly remarkable given the intensity of cultural conditioning about women's bodies and the various sanctions for non-conformity. Like many others, Sandra Bartky has noted that the notion of "the perfect female body" is reinforced daily in media images of femininity, leaving no doubt in most women's minds of their deficiency in this area (Bartky, 1990, pp. 71–72). Despite the unattainable nature of such prescriptions for most women, in her view their influence is great precisely because they speak to the core of female identity:

> To have a body felt to be feminine, i.e., a body constructed through the appropriate practices, is crucial in most cases to a woman's sense of herself as female and, since, in the binary system in which we appear to be trapped, every person must be either male or female, to her sense of herself as an existing individual.
>
> (Bartky, 1998, p. 24)

If the norms of femininity "are importantly implicated in the very construction of our subjectivities" (Bartky, 1998, p. 24), it is not hard to see that rational decisions or intentions to refuse them capture only one aspect of what is involved in their destabilization. What is particularly insightful in Foucault's analysis of the type of power operating in modern societies is precisely its illumination of what is at stake in attempts to constitute ourselves differently. If we accept his claim that individuals are to a large extent governed through deeply ingrained practices of self-policing, we are less likely to fall into the trap of underestimating the power of dominant self-understandings. If certain commonly accepted ideas about what it means to be a woman, a man, a mother, a child, a sexual being, a person of moral worth, a success, and so forth fashion our experience of selfhood and provide the basis by which others judge us and we judge ourselves, it is not difficult to see that a simple act of will is unlikely to transform ill-fitting norms. Appreciating this helps make sense of the way individuals participate in their own oppression. It also counters the power of derogatory ideas about women being their own worst enemy when preferred identities are underperformed.

OTHER WAYS OF KNOWING

In the therapeutic context, it is possible to weaken the disempowering effects of privileging the rational by exploring different types of knowing – physical, emotional, psychological, spiritual and intellectual – and connections between these. As Johnella Bird argues: "When we negotiate the meanings attributed to significant life events by utilising the resources of ideas, feelings and the body, we access a richer tapestry of potential meanings" (Bird, 2000, p. 18). Self-policing tends to manifest in the form of negative thoughts – for example in voices of self-criticism, self-hate or self-doubt. This type of thinking, however, is not restricted to the category of a discrete intellectual understanding. Rather it tends to reverberate throughout one's being inflicting blows to the body, emotions, psyche and spirit. Once the apparent naturalness of self-policing has been disturbed, it becomes possible to undermine its power further by finding language that touches the spirit, the heart and the body. This is not to underestimate the usefulness of thinking through alternative ideas. Rather it is a reminder that when these ideas challenge deeply embedded cultural norms and are tied to the maintenance of given power relations, a purely intellectual decision to embody new ideas and practices is unlikely to be the only component of change. Such a reminder helps clarify what women frequently are up against in efforts to move beyond given norms. When it is recognized that the difficulties entailed do not speak of personal deficit, there is greater freedom to resist unwanted norms and to do so in ways that are compassionate to and enhancing of the self.

TOWARDS A MORE HOLISTIC CONCEPTION OF CARE

The dualist tendency of western thought also is reflected in the dichotomizing of caring relations into two distinct, gender-related types of activity. As noted, within this dichotomy women's primary responsibility for nurture has tended to orient them more towards others than the self. Conversely, male socialization processes have encouraged a greater focus on the self and the expectation that this will be supported by girls and women. A focus on women's responsibility for nurture is not to deny the reality of men's care for others as, for example, exhibited in historical breadwinner and protector roles.[6] Unlike the latter, however, and despite its key social role, women's caring has been attributed the customary devaluation associated with the emotional and feminine. This also can be understood in light of the cultural primacy of notions of autonomous, rational and separate selves. Indeed the qualities of interconnectedness and particularity required for the provision of emotional nurturance are diametrically opposite to those traditionally associated with the privileged masculine self; that is, autonomy and a capacity for objective generalized reasoning. The effects for women of the sexual division of caring can include a lack of adequate care from others, the normalizing of uncaring relations and a lack of ease in receiving care from others and/or the self (see Jordan *et al.*, 1991, pp. 153, 30). Conversely, if a dichotomous notion of care was replaced by a holistic conception characterized by an inextricable link between giving and receiving, women would be more likely to feel uneasy if they were *not* the recipients of care. Conceived thus, care for the self becomes an integral aspect of the general notion of care. Moreover, within such a notion caring for others becomes a valued activity for which we are all responsible. As Barry Smart argues "[i]t is only possible for care for self to encompass care for others if there is from the beginning, if there is *already*, a responsibility for the other" (Smart, 1998, p. 87). A holistic notion of care cuts across the sexual division of caring and creates space for the acknowledgement of care as a crucial and desirable aspect of human existence. When caring ceases to play a role in women's (or anyone's) subordination, the full vitality of its creative capacity to structure human relations can flourish.

SUMMARY

This chapter proposed that greater care for the self in women's lives can undermine the power of self-policing. The latter keeps women tied to a strict overseer type of self-relationship in the service of given identity practices, standards and norms. Drawing on aspects of Foucault's later work, I argued that an emphasis on the type of ethical relationship we have with ourselves provides a way of redressing an imbalance in many women's lives between care for the self and care for others. The type of care for the self advocated by Foucault involves creative interaction with given relations of power in order to actively participate in the fashioning of different identities. While this aspect of his thought promises to be fruitful, McNay's critique helps to highlight limitations of the ancient structure of self-relations on which he draws. In thinking about a type of relationship with the self more likely to undermine self-policing and facilitate the type of creative identity-making advocated by Foucault, I suggested the usefulness of hooks' notion of structuring relationships around the principle of love and Lugones' concept of playfulness. A fuller articulation of alternative attitudes to the self was presented in the section on friendship with the self.

Prior to this, McNay's concern about the viability of Foucault's claim that proper care for the self will prevent the domination of others was discussed. I argued that in light of women's predominantly other-oriented training this may be more of a problem generally in relation to males. This is not to imply that women's training is unmediated by factors of race, class or sexuality or that this is unproblematic. It is rather to acknowledge the significance of one's caring relations for the self in the development of ethical relations with others. In thinking about ways in which greater care for the self might be operationalized, I advocated the value of friendship as an organizing principle in relations with the self. In the therapeutic context, I suggested the practice of relating to the self as one would to a friend as one way of facilitating this type of friendship.

Towards the end of the chapter, I looked at the way in which the cultural privileging of our rational capacities understates the emotional, involuntary and/or psychic dimensions often entailed in the refashioning of identities. This can encourage a sense of failure when preferred practices of the self are underperformed. Following McNay, it was argued that particularly when self-fashioning involves movement away from deeply entrenched cultural norms and the maintenance of social hierarchies, a simple act of rational intention is unlikely to be the only component of change. In the therapeutic context, this can be affirmed by exploring knowledges of the body, emotions, mind and spirit. Finally, I pointed to the need for a less dichotomous conception of care which cuts across the sexual division of caring by encompassing both the notion of giving and receiving.

An emphasis on greater care for the self in women's lives is not to ignore the continuing presence of broader social structures and practices which perpetuate subordination and call for political resistance and change at the macro-level. Rather it is argued that enhanced care for the self provides a way of refusing the intra-subjective effects of assigned identities. In this light, it can be seen as constituting political activity at the "micro-physical" level. This is not to privilege this type of political action over others. It is merely a claim that the personal is one level at which it is possible and desirable to effect progressive social change. Moreover, the idea of enhanced self-care in women's lives is compatible with one of feminism's primary goals to develop women's sense of their own value as a necessary basis for the existence of an oppositional movement. In this regard, Sawicki draws a parallel between Foucault's notion of the critical subject who is capable of reflecting historically, refusing given accounts of identity and creatively inventing others, and that which informs the feminist practice of consciousness-raising (Sawicki, 1991, pp. 103–104, 106).

Foucault's thought has featured strongly in the discussion of self-policing and greater care for the self. At the beginning of Chapter 3 it also is listed as one of the key influences in narrative therapy. The next chapter addresses the issue of whether narrative therapy's use of Foucauldian ideas is legitimate. It also outlines the influence of two other schools of thought which supplement Foucault's contribution.

6

FOUCAULT AND THERAPY – A CONTRADICTION?

INTRODUCTION

This chapter discusses the use of Foucault's thought in the context of therapy. While the application of this thought to the therapeutic domain may strike some readers as paradoxical, perhaps even contradictory, I argue that narrative therapy remains within the spirit of Foucault's endeavour. Foucault's challenge to the necessary nature of Enlightenment rationality inspires a critique of taken-for-granted therapeutic assumptions. This gives rise to the development of practices which assist people to resist the power of scientific "truths" to define their experience and identity and encourage the exploration and performance of alternative understandings. Rather than involving the discovery of a "true" or essential identity, re-authoring always takes place in relation to a set of sociohistorical practices. It is argued that by undermining the power of therapeutic discourse to impose an essential identity, narrative therapy subverts rather than perpetuates privileged notions of selfhood. In a parallel move to Foucault, the problematizing of therapeutic realities makes it more difficult for those authorized by professional discourses to continue to speak and act in characteristic ways. Discussion of the legitimacy of using Foucault's thought in this domain concludes by reference to two strands of critique from within family therapy literature. Finally, I point to the important contributions of two other influences on the development of narrative therapy.

FOUCAULT AND THERAPY

Given that narrative therapy is informed significantly by Foucauldian ideas,[1] the issue of the legitimacy of their application to the therapeutic domain needs to be addressed. At first blush, the linking of Foucault's thought to therapy may appear paradoxical given his challenge to forms of knowledge that have constructed categories of illness, pathology, and so on. This is borne out most forcefully in his early study of the various social constructions of madness since the Middle Ages, which ends with an account of its confinement within mental illness in the modern era, entrusted to the discipline of psychiatry. Moreover, in this work Foucault begins an ongoing debate with Sigmund Freud and psychoanalysis (Foucault, 1967). In *The History of Sexuality Volume 1* he points to the illusory nature of the liberatory promises of therapies like psychoanalysis, claiming that through their instillation of the urge to confess such therapies actually produce self-policing persons tied to a restricted notion of identity (Foucault, 1978). In his final works, the Freudian notion of self becomes the main target of his endeavour to reproblematize selfhood, particularly in relation to his historical investigation of desire (Bernauer, 1992, p. 167).

Yet Foucault disputed the claim that he was opposed to psychiatry: "I have done nothing other than write the history of psychiatry to the beginning of the 19th century. Why should so many people, including psychiatrists, believe that I am an anti-psychiatrist?" (Kritzman, 1988, p. 15). In his view, this false inference is drawn because "they are not able to accept the real history of their institutions" (Kritzman, 1988, p. 15). Rather than aligning himself with the anti-psychiatry movement, his aim is to make it more problematic for those authorized by therapeutic discourses to continue to speak and act in characteristic ways. This is the general stance he adopts in his historical analyses. Thus, in relation to the subsequent work on punishment, he explicitly states his intention

> to bring it about that . . . those who work in the institutional setting of the prison . . . "no longer know what to do", so that the acts, gestures, discourses which up until then had seemed to go without saying become problematic, difficult, dangerous.
>
> (Foucault, 1991, p. 84)

This reflects his view that the intellectual's task is not to sketch aims or prescribe truths but rather

> to question over and over again what is postulated as self-evident, to disturb people's mental habits, the way they do and think things, to dissipate what is familiar and accepted, to reexamine rules and institutions and on the basis of this reproblematization . . . to participate in the formation of a political will.
>
> (Kritzman, 1988, p. 265)

Moreover, in an interview shortly before his death, Foucault refutes the criticism that the logic of his position regarding the existence of different historical "truths" about madness means that madness does not exist. For him, it is precisely a question of understanding how madness, defined in its various ways, can at a particular historical moment be incorporated into an institutional arena which views it as mental illness, holding a certain position alongside other illnesses (Foucault, 1988, pp. 9–10, 17).

In the spirit of disturbing established "truths", narrative therapy takes as its starting point the problematization of commonly accepted ideas and practices in the therapeutic domain. It seeks to render the familiar strange and contestable, thereby clearing a space for a considered rearticulation of ideas and practices. In this light, its use of Foucauldian thought is not as paradoxical as may first appear.

A second concern about linking Foucault's work with narrative therapy could derive from the latter's clear commitment to a notion of social justice and to emancipatory projects. Such notions may seem to sit uneasily with the emphasis in Foucault's best known works on the insidious nature of a disciplinary power more focused on the efficient operation of the modern status quo than on redressing its injustices. Yet it is not hard to see similarities between Foucault's identification with the downtrodden and oppressed in his historical analyses (Bernauer, 1992, p. 182) and narrative therapy's social justice focus. Such a focus reflects an awareness of the degree to which the problems people experience may be caught up in social structures of inequality. The notion of emancipatory projects, moreover, is prominent in Foucault's later work. While such a notion usually is associated with modernist projects, Foucault extends the emancipatory concern of earlier thought through explicit avoidance of any notion of an a priori essence which needs to be freed from repressive relations of power. In his view, maximizing possibilities for human freedom includes being able to interrogate the idea of an essential identity and actively participating in the making and re-making of ourselves (McNay, 1992, pp. 5, 62, 84, 89–90). Viewed in this light, the use of Foucault's work in developing a therapeutic approach which disturbs taken-for-granted notions of identity and relationship, and actively encourages individuals, families and groups to take part in defining who they are, can be seen to reside within the spirit of his thought. This claim is fleshed out in the following text.

UNIVERSAL KNOWLEDGE CLAIMS

Foucault's claim for the contingency of modern scientific discourse provides an impetus for critiquing key therapeutic assumptions, including the notion of an authentic self and certain claims about the nature of this self and about the formation and resolution of problems (White, 1997, Ch. 1, pp. 119–120). As in all modern disciplines, such claims are legitimated by appeal to an objective and universal reason. As White expresses this view,

> The professional disciplines have been successful in the development of language practices and techniques that determine that it is those disciplines that have access to the "truth" of the world. These techniques encourage persons in the belief that the members of these disciplines have access to an objective and unbiased account of reality, and of human nature.
>
> (White, 1991, p. 36)

For White, the perception of professional discourses as rational and neutral and their emphasis on the authoritative and impersonal expert position places them in the category referred to by Foucault as "global and unitary" accounts of knowledge (Gordon, 1980, pp. 80–81). As such, the historical conflicts that have accompanied their movement towards dominant status are obscured, including the many resistances to them, and questions about their cultural, political and historical context are precluded. In this way, the elevation of expert knowledge claims to the status of truth tends to discourage reflection on their ethical implications. The latter include perpetuating the structures of privilege and power relations of the broader culture. In the therapeutic discipline this, in turn, can marginalize those seeking assistance, reinforce knowledge hierarchies, discount other types of thought and life, maintain the therapist's power monopoly and render invisible her or his embodied social location. Once the truth status of dominant knowledges is disturbed, however, the possibility of examining their effects on recipients of therapy increases (White, 1991, p. 37; 1997, pp. 122–123). In White's view, a prime candidate for this type of investigation is the central discourse of pathology:

> The word makes me wince! When I hear it, I think about the spectacular success of clinical medicine in the objectification of persons and of their bodies, and the extent to which the pathologising of persons is the most common and taken-for-granted practice in the mental health/welfare disciplines, and the central and most major achievement of the psychologies.
>
> (White, 1995, p. 112)

Charles Waldegrave argues that despite its widely accepted use, the sickness/pathology analogy is not a neutral category but rather a therapeutic creation specifying a certain status, ability and set of expectations (Waldegrave, 1990, p. 12). Indicating the possibility of a very different meaning of problematic experience, he depicts the so-called "presenting problem" as a sacred story imparted in trust rather than a pathology requiring treatment; this gives a spiritual quality to the therapeutic exchange that moves it beyond the realm of clinical science:

> People come to therapy and make themselves vulnerable by
> exposing the deepest and most personal events in their lives, along
> with their explanations of those events. They often feel defeated
> and even humiliated by the persistence of their problem. In these
> circumstances their exposing of their pain and the context out of
> which it springs, is like a gift, a very personal offering, to the
> therapist: it has a spiritual quality. This offering is worthy of
> honour. It is not a scientific pathology that requires removal, nor is
> it an ill-informed understanding of the problem that requires
> correction. It is, rather, a person's articulation of events and the
> meaning given to those events which have become problematic.
>
> (Waldegrave, 1990, p. 33)

In reflecting on the dominance of models of pathology, White refers to the
great incentives for mental health professionals to demonstrate "diagnostic
acumen" in terms of their professional career structures. He claims that in
the USA it is increasingly almost mandatory for mental health professionals
to subject their work to the official manual of diagnoses in order to earn a
living. Moreover, since pathology discourses claim access to objective
truth, consequences of the ways in which professionals talk about and
interact with the people who consult them are rendered invisible. In this
way, these discourses encourage a lack of accountability and reinforce and
extend the power of mental health professionals. Pathologizing discourses
also allow professionals to ignore the degree to which people's daily living
conditions may contribute to their problem experiences (White, 1995, pp.
114–115). Conversely, as Ian Law argues, if the notion of objective truth is
destabilized therapists are faced with a choice of which perspective to
privilege: "to search for pathology; to attempt a position of neutrality,
which usually means becoming complicit with dominant pathologising
culture; or alternatively to bring pathologising descriptions themselves into
question" (Law, 1998b, p. 192).

If the latter route is taken, it becomes harder for mental health professionals to ignore the extent to which the problems people experience
often are caught up in cultural structures of inequality.[2] White argues that
to see people's problems as the product of some aberration rather than of
our ways of thinking and living makes it possible to avoid addressing
professional complicity in perpetuating these forms of thought and life
(White, 1995, pp. 115–116). In his view, when the experience and
context of everyday life, the diversity of understandings of this, and the
real effects of these understandings are brought into focus, contestation
emerges as the condition of life. When this is acknowledged "the politics
of inequality and marginalization, of oppression and subjugation, of
dominance and submission, of exploitation and resistance" (White, 1995,
p. 217) are brought to the fore. This enables "[t]he struggles around

gender, class, race, ethnicity, age, and sexual orientation [to] demand acknowledgment" (White, 1995, p. 217). Such a view contrasts with the conventional family therapy emphasis on stability and equilibrium as the norm (White, 1995, pp. 214–215, 217).

POWER/KNOWLEDGE

Foucault's notion of the inseparability of knowledge and power provides a coherent rationale for investigating the concrete effects, risks and limitations of dominant therapeutic ideas and practice. Such a notion directly challenges the idea of a neutral standpoint from which objective truth claims can be made. The idea that we all are enmeshed in networks of power and knowledge (albeit not equally in terms of their effects) enables a break from the conventional view that knowledge is problematic only when used corruptly by those in power. A further useful aspect of Foucault's notion of the indissociability of knowledge and power is that it removes this type of critique from the realm of the good intentions or otherwise of mental health professionals and institutions and focuses instead on the rules underlying those knowledges which have attained dominant status (White and Epston, 1990, pp. 22, 29). From this perspective, the best of intentions may be found to have disabling or marginalizing effects.

THE PRODUCTIVE CAPACITY OF POWER

Foucault's notion of power as a productive rather than merely repressive force offers a new perspective in relation to therapy. His analysis of the constitution and government of modern identity provides a framework for thinking about the broader cultural context within which dominant therapeutic ideas and practices are located. This, in turn, inspires ways of thinking about how subjugating aspects of the dominant culture may be being reproduced in the therapeutic interaction to the detriment of those seeking assistance. As such, it encourages a general questioning of issues of politics and power. Moreover, Foucault's identification of Bentham's Panopticon as the "ideal" model for an economic and positive form of power helps explain how people have been recruited into "collaborating in the subjugation of their own lives and in the objectification of their own bodies; . . . how they became 'willing' participants in the disciplining of, or policing of, their own lives" (White, 1991, pp. 34–35). White argues that if it is accepted that power's global effects are assured by its operations at the micro-level of social life and the margins of society, then joining with people to challenge practices of power which tie them to ill-fitting identity prescriptions is a political act; it is also a political act not to do so (White and Epston, 1990, pp. 18–20, 28–29).

NORMALIZING POWER

Foucault's analysis also provides a framework for critiquing the disempowering effects of certain routine practices. His identification of the bureaucratic "file" as a strategy of power is one example (Foucault, 1979). White argues that traditionally the file or casenote has played a key role in facilitating social control and subjugation. Having assumed an independent life, the file totalizes (frequently in deficit terms) the person to which it refers (White, 1995, pp. 46–47). He depicts the conventional recording of hospital casenotes as:

> a practice that contributes significantly to [an] experience of "otherness", and one that reinforces some of the very negative stories of identity that are experienced by so many of these people. It is a practice that plays a significant part in modern rituals of degradation.
>
> (White, 1995, p. 168)

Entailed in this process is an appropriation of the experience of the person seeking assistance and its transformation into the language of expert knowledge. In challenging such a practice White and Epston suggest that, if note taking is deemed to be helpful, it should be drawn from information which emphasizes people's particular knowledges and skills and their place in the broader community. Moreover, while the traditional file tends to be limited to the readership of professionals, this alternative form of documentation can be made available both to the person to whom it refers and, if they wish, to significant others in their community (White and Epston, 1990, pp. 189–190). An example of the effects of these differing approaches to note taking is recounted by Jill Freedman and Gene Combs:

> [The woman] said that when she read her hospital chart she felt old and small and stuck. She felt like a chronic mental patient with no hope, not even like a person. Then she talked about reading Michael White's notes. She said that the more she read the more alive she felt. She could see movement in her life. She felt like a valuable person who was making her life better every day.
>
> (Freedman and Combs, 1996, p. 207)

A further "counter-practice" advocated by White is turning the intense and objectifying gaze to which people's lives are subject back on itself. One example of this in the psychiatric context would be for those subjected to ward rounds to undertake a study of the conditions that make this practice possible. This could include asking who is authorized to speak, what are the circumstances in which they can speak, which ways of speaking are recognized and which disqualified, whose voice is privileged, what are the effects of this privileging, and so forth. He has found that even if this idea is not taken up formally its mere introduction can have an empowering effect: "It appears that even to think the unthinkable goes some way towards undoing the effects of the marginalisation to which people have been subject" (White, 1995, pp. 122–123). Moreover, because turning the gaze back on itself can render many taken-for-granted psychiatric ideas and practices visible, it can be of assistance to mental health professionals committed to taking ethical responsibility for the concrete effects of their work (White, 1995, p. 123).

NOTIONS OF SELFHOOD

The normalizing gaze of modernity is nowhere more penetrating than in relation to notions of identity. In this regard, Foucault's account of the ways in which certain practices of power are disguised in the form of promises of fulfilment or liberation speaks to White's experience. Having witnessed the debilitating and restrictive effects of various popular discourses that incite people to measure themselves against conceptions of "ideal" and "natural" ways of being, narrative therapy explicitly does not aim to assist people

> to be truly who they really are, but, in fact, [to] free them from the "real", . . . [assisting them] to resist the great incitement of popular psychology to tyrannise ourselves into a state of "authenticity", . . . to refuse "wholeness", to protest "personal growth", to usurp the various states of "realness". To open the possibilities . . . to default, and to break from the sort of gymnastics that regulate these states of being, that make all of this possible.
> (White, 1995, p. 48)[3]

This echoes Foucault's view that there is no essential self that gets distorted by practices of power: "it is not that the beautiful totality of the individual is amputated, repressed, altered by our social order, it is rather that the individual is carefully fabricated in it, according to a whole technique of forces and bodies" (Foucault, 1979, p. 217). By seeking to illuminate the cost of popular aspirations for selfhood – that liberation efforts which seek to uncover a true self obscured by forces of repression bind people ever more tightly to taken-for-granted notions of individuality – narrative therapy clears a space for people to become "other than they are". In this way it echoes the type of thinking and practice advocated by Foucault. It might be argued that this approach nonetheless remains within the archetypal confessional discipline which he depicts as the modern manifestation of an older form of coercion (Foucault, 1978, pp. 130–131). Yet the target of his critique of the therapeutic domain appears to be a traditional psychoanalytic version of the self. At a very fundamental level this entails "a basic sense of self which is constituted at an early age and continues into adult life cutting across divisions of race, class and ethnicity" (McNay, 1992, p. 9). In challenging such a notion, narrative therapy undermines the power of therapeutic discourse to impose an essential identity. This opens up possibilities for exploring ways of thinking and being in the world which lie beyond culturally venerated ideas about human nature and which illuminate the dynamic and ongoing nature of identity formation (White, 1997, pp. 224–227; 2002).

In a discussion about appropriate medical services, Foucault's concern is for the establishment of a non-dominatory system: "The problem is to know how one may actually obtain therapeutic results, which it would be pitiful to deny, without the setting up of a type of medical power, and a type of relationship to the body, and a type of authoritarianism – a *system of obedience*" (Kritzman, 1988, p. 195). Similarly, in the therapeutic context, it is not a question of denying assistance but rather of creating an environment which challenges commonly accepted practices of power and fosters active participation in identity-making. When this occurs, the therapeutic domain has the potential to subvert rather than perpetuate taken-for-granted realities. This has been demonstrated in relation to various therapies including psychoanalysis.[4]

THE THERAPEUTIC RELATIONSHIP

The therapeutic relationship itself also provides an arena for disturbing commonplaces. Here Foucault's insistence on the inevitable presence of power in human relationships is seen as an important safeguard. If therapists acknowledge the existence of a power relationship, they are more likely to seek actively to minimize its toxic effects (White, 1995, pp. 175–176; 2000, pp. 136–137).[5] This is particularly important given that the therapeutic relationship is usually entered into at a time of heightened vulnerability on the part of the person(s) seeking assistance. Yet it is an area where the need for such reflection, apart from that referring to explicit exploitation by the therapist, is easily overlooked by notions of good intentions and commitment to helping people. As Rachel Hare-Mustin points out, therapy tends to reflect dominant interests and values, and discourses associated with members of subordinate gender, race, class and sexuality groups are likely to be excluded from the therapy room. When conformity to dominant notions of identity and relationship are put forward as the only possible option, not only does this close down other possibilities which may suit people better but it actually can subject them to the same type of practices that already have been destructive. Good intentions notwithstanding, therefore, if the goals pursued by therapists are left unquestioned, they can be acting as agents of social control in attempts to impose normalizing behaviour on those seeking assistance (Hare-Mustin, 1994, pp. 20–21). In White's view, this means that a commitment to helping people requires thinking about the different ways in which therapy may be reproducing the dominant culture:

> It is never a matter of whether or not we bring politics (of class, race, sexuality, age, etc.) into the therapy room, but it is a matter of whether or not we are prepared to acknowledge the existence of these politics, and it is a matter of the degree to which we are prepared to be complicit in the reproduction of these politics.
>
> (White, 1994a, p. 1)

THE ROLE OF THE INTELLECTUAL

In Foucault's view, part of the political work of the intellectual is to understand power's operations in a particular society: "their historical formation, the source of their strength or fragility, the conditions which are necessary to transform some or to abolish others" (Foucault, 1982, p. 223). This entails rendering strange taken-for-granted ideas and practices in specific social domains with the aim of generating a "community of action" to participate in contesting the limits in question. Foucault is concerned to dissociate himself from the model which promotes the intellectual as representing a universal voice or conscience. Rather he champions the notion of the "specific intellectual" who makes no absolute truth and justice claims and who is deeply committed to understanding the particular power dynamics of her or his institutions of work in order to facilitate a critique and rearticulation of policy. He also is reluctant to advocate specific solutions or a progressive framework or programme; he is too aware of how such programmes can be used as tools of oppression (Rabinow, 1984, pp. 67–68, 73–74, 46–47, 375, 385). Moreover, to provide solutions or blueprints goes against his view that people need to construct their own ethics (Kritzman, 1988, p. 16).

The type of critique undertaken by narrative therapy is compatible with the "specific intellectual" model advocated by Foucault. This is reflected in its investigation of the specific power effects of expert knowledge claims in the domain of therapy. It also examines the ways in which cultural divisions of race, class, gender, sexuality, health, age, and so on may be reproduced in the therapeutic context. Echoing Foucault's conviction that power's global hold is assured by its operations at the local level, White and Epston develop practices which subvert the power of dominant discourses to define people's identities and lives. This creates space for the exploration and performance of notions of identity and relationship over which people have more say. In White's view, this goes some way towards realizing Foucault's call for liberation from commonly accepted notions of what it means to be human and the promotion of new modes of sub-jectivity (White and Epston, 1990, p. 75). Finally, narrative therapy's critique has led to the formation of a community of therapists which seeks to illuminate and expand the limits of its discipline.

EMANCIPATORY PROJECTS

The incorporation of both a deconstructive and reconstructive emphasis in Foucault's thought is paralleled in narrative therapy. In re-authoring work, the influence of his continued emphasis on the lack of inevitability of modern identity modes remains significant. First, it is through such a notion that the given nature of problematic experience and identity can be challenged. This entails exploring the historical and cultural limits that have constituted people as they are and reflection on whether these limits are in line with their own preferences. In turn, this type of investigation creates space for the development and performance of alternative iden-tities. Re-authored identities emerge from an exploration of neglected or inarticulated meanings and experiences hitherto obscured by dominant, "problem-saturated" self and other understandings (White and Epston, 1990, pp. 31–32, 56). As noted, this does not point to the recovery of a true or essential self. Foucault refers to the way in which such a notion has at times underpinned programmes at the broad political level and in institutions such as the asylum and the prison, with disastrous effects (Darier, 1996, pp. 8–9). Working for many years in the psychiatric system, White and Epston have witnessed the often demoralizing and tragic effects of people being treated in line with certain "truths" about human nature. For this reason they are not inclined to situate their practices within discourses that "assert objective reality accounts of the human condition" (White and Epston, 1990, p. 28). This corresponds with Foucault's claim that our relationship to the self does not have to be informed by scientific knowledge (Rabinow, 1984, pp. 349–350). Situating re-authoring work within the sociohistorical context undercuts the power of essentialist versions of the self to determine identity and opens up possibilities for creative, multiple and open-ended self-making (White, 1997, pp. 54–55, 231–232). As such, re-authoring projects are compatible with Foucault's aim "to give new impetus . . . to the undefined work of freedom" (Rabinow, 1984, p. 46). Finally, Foucault's call for an ethos of self-critique and the investigation of new forms of subjectivity counters any argument that the discipline of therapy *inevitably* serves coercive purposes. As Lois McNay notes, his later work on practices of the self offers a way of escaping the vicious cycle in which resistance inevitably leads back to domination (McNay, 1992, p. 87).

FAMILY THERAPY CRITIQUES

I now turn to two strands of critique of narrative therapy's use of Foucault from within the family therapy literature. One strand questions the validity of using Foucault's work, understood as a purely critical and deconstructionist tool, in the development of a different type of therapy. In one argument of this kind, this is precluded because in Foucault's schema "[t]here is, simply, no 'outside' to th[e] reality of the constitution of subjectivity" (Luepnitz, 1992, p. 282). This type of critique echoes some of the general interpretive debates about Foucault's thought. What it ignores, however, is the emphasis in his later work on investigating strategies of freedom available in social relationships (Rabinow, 1984, p. 48). Moreover, while it is true to say that for Foucault there is no position beyond the constitution of subjectivity, this does not imply the existence of only one form of subjectivity from which all identities are fashioned. As David Hoy argues, genealogy conceives humans as standing in multiple communities simultaneously, each of which emerges from varying contingencies. This means that while it is not possible to make judgements about a particular set of social practices from some neutral position, we can do so from the standpoint of other self-descriptions we know to be feasible (Hoy, 1998, p. 30). Indeed this fits with the description of Foucault's work as a tool of critique. If, however, we can criticize and deconstruct social practices from the viewpoint of alternative self-understandings, presumably those understandings also imply alternative possibilities for thinking and living. It is precisely this type of argument that has been levelled against the absence of an explicit normative framework in Foucault's genealogies (see Fraser, 1989, pp. 18–19, 29–31, 57; Taylor, 1984). Emancipatory ideas do not come from a point beyond history or culture but are present or have their potential in existing social discourses.

A second strand of critique is expressed by Vincent Fish (1993). Fish sees narrative therapy as committing the un-Foucauldian act of privileging individual experience and implying that altering a personal narrative is the same as changing a cultural discourse. In response to such a claim, Fred Redekop warns against the polarization of personal narrative and cultural discourse in Foucault's work. He points to Foucault's re-publication of the memoirs of the nineteenth-century French hermaphrodite Hercules Barbin and the parricide Pierre Rivière in which he gives primacy to their personal accounts and contextualizes these within the prescribed knowledges of the day. Redekop describes similar processes of cultural contextualization and "re-publication" of personal stories in narrative therapy. This refutes a further charge by Fish that narrative therapy fails to address the local use of power. In terms of the issue of its position in relation to the therapeutic domain, Redekop identifies a Foucauldian concern to problematize the ways in which one's perspective or field conditions the type of questions that tend to be pursued (Redekop, 1995).

Some further points can be made in relation to Fish's concern about the difference between altering a personal story and changing a discourse. He claims that

> changing a destructive narrative to a more positive narrative *within the same cultural discourse* is not identical to getting free of that cultural discourse. Nor does it have anything to do with altering the discourse itself in the way that Foucault envisioned an "insurrection of knowledges" might accomplish.
>
> (Fish, 1993, p. 223)

Before addressing Fish's specific focus on mental illness, such claims generally appear to ignore the link between identity formation and privileged cultural discourse. If it is accepted that identity is constituted in relation to a set of sociohistorical practices and if it is also the case, as both Foucault and narrative therapy argue, that other ways of understanding ourselves can be generated and enacted, narrative therapy's claim to assist people to subvert the influence of oppressive discourses is legitimate. As Hoy argues, this does not require a point of neutrality beyond culture. Rather it is possible to extricate ourselves from an oppressive discourse through engaging with another discourse from within the same culture. Following Redekop, this can be illustrated through an example of White's work with a man who had been violent to his family. This man was encouraged to examine the influence of culturally dominant beliefs on his view of himself as a man, how he had been recruited into living according to these beliefs and their effects on his life and relationships. As the work evolved, he experienced a move away from previously familiar and taken-for-granted views and practices towards an exploration and performance of alternative relationship practices (White, 1991, pp. 25–26, 36). This process involved becoming free of the influence of certain cultural discourses – for example those privileging men's authority within the family and attributing proprietorial rights over family members, including the right to inflict harm and sexual entitlement – which provide the framework within which abusive behaviour is made possible. This is not to imply that all men are abusive but rather that the potential for abuse exists in the social privileging of certain gender discourses.

While not all men who abuse will choose to step away from this behaviour, change at the individual level plays a crucial role in the struggle against domestic violence. If Foucault is correct to claim that power's effectiveness is guaranteed through its operations at the local level, altering a discourse must include intra-personal change. This is not to deny the need for other levels of change. As Clare O'Farrell argues:

> The modification of the self (a self which does not exist prior to society or history) produces a modification of one's activity in relation to others, and hence a modification in power relations, even if only at the micro-level to begin with. Thus Foucault's position certainly does not lead to the refusal of political or social action.
>
> (O'Farrell, 1989, p. 129)

Rather, an understanding of the way one has been fashioned and fashions oneself sociohistorically is an important component of broader social change (O'Farrell, 1989, p. 129). Thus, while legislation which criminalizes domestic violence importantly signals the community's moral and legal opposition to family violence, this alone is insufficient to alter "the culturally constructed and mediated sense of entitlement and righteousness than can enable men to feel justified in using practices of domination and control in relation to others" (Law, 1998a, p. 121). As indicated, in White's experience a crucial aspect of working with men who have abused their partners and/or children is developing a context which allows them to separate their sense of identity from the taken-for-granted ideas and practices that provide a framework for the abuse and to explore alternative possibilities for relationship (White, 1995, pp. 159–160). Moreover, when such change occurs its effects can extend beyond the individuals concerned. This is particularly significant in terms of interrupting the possibility (though not inevitability) of generational patterns of violence and abuse by exposing children to a different model of relationship practices. In the context of women and the family, Joan Laird points to the creative dynamic between individual change and the strengthening of preferred local narratives:

> Just as gaining the power to influence social discourse and social meanings can bring about change on the societal level, so the restorying process on the individual or family level offers powerful potential for change, not just for the individuals involved but in imitating and strengthening alternative local knowledges. For example, as the women's movement has helped to shape our

113

consciousness concerning the patriarchal nature of the traditional family, so many individual women, strengthened by feminism, have restoried and restructured their family lives in very important ways.

(Laird, 1994, p. 182)

Moreover, the re-storying of individual experiences of child abuse and violence is helping to reshape broader social understandings of these practices (Laird, 1994, p. 195).

Fish's specific concern in relation to the difference between altering a personal narrative and a cultural discourse is about re-authoring work with those deemed mentally ill. He describes such work as politically conservative in terms of its potential to reinforce dominant discourses about normality and mental illness (Fish, 1993, p. 223). Such a claim, however, is at odds with narrative therapy's professed commitment to working with people to identify conventional notions of health and normality, and their associated expectations, in order that they might develop resistance strategies to the negative effects of these conceptions. This also enables an exploration of the parts of people's lives they may be able to appreciate which defy these conceptions (White, 1995, pp. 139–140). Evidence of this type of work is reflected in the experiences of a group of people who live with destructive voices and visions. The "Power to Our Journeys" group emphasizes the importance of narrative therapy's provision of a space in which to expose the workings and tactics of these voices and visions. This contrasts with their experiences of other therapeutic contexts:

We have been silenced time and again by many psychiatric professionals who have consistently refused to acknowledge our experiences of these voices and visions . . . [T]his silencing has profoundly negative consequences for all of our lives . . . At times this very silencing has contributed to a sense that we might be going mad . . . We cannot . . . emphasise strongly enough how important it is to have the opportunity to speak of the troublesome voices and visions in a forum that contributes to a powerful exposé of their purpose and their operations.

(Brigitte et al., 1997, pp. 26–27)

This type of exposé enables a revision of people's relationship with the voices and visions in which the extent of the latter's influence is reduced. This process also involves enlisting the assistance of supportive, or potentially supportive, voices which may exist alongside destructive ones or which may be resurrected "invisible" childhood friends. The approach to both destructive and supportive voices undermines the conventional idea that voices heard by people are aspects of themselves they need to integrate. Underlying such a notion is the view that humans are self-contained beings characterized by a single essence which contains the core and source of all meaning (White, 1995, pp. 124, 127, 132–138). For members of the "Power to Our Journeys" group, developing a revised relationship with the voices and visions, and their work together, has contributed to an ability to step outside "normal" values and expectations:

> we have all experienced a change in our position on traditional materialistic values. It is not that we have dispensed with all materialistic values, it is just that they no longer mean what they meant to us previously . . . This means that many of our old associations with happiness no longer mean much to us. Instead, it is the lightness of being that we experience from moment to moment that matters most to us. And it is the mischievousness that we find becoming more and more a part of our everyday sense of our lives, of our humour, that is important. We even are able to embrace the fact that, in many ways, we stand outside of what is expected of people in our culture, and to poke fun at these expectations. At these times we feel like larrikins, and the feeling is just great. All this means that on those occasions when we feel at risk of again being caught up in a tempest, we don't quite lose sight of the sun.
>
> (Brigette *et al.*, 1997, p. 28)

Such achievements surely perturb cultural discourses about mental illness and normality. Central to the notion of normality is the ability to exercise control over one's thoughts and actions. The conscious decision of members of the "Power to Our Journeys" group to place themselves beyond the constraining nature of certain taken-for-granted cultural expectations is at odds with such a clear cut delineation between well-being and illness. As well as providing an important defence in the struggle against destructive voices and visions, this ability points to certain freedoms often less available to those deemed normal. This brings to mind Foucault's concern about the loss associated with modernity's silencing of the powers of "unreason" that question our taken-for-granted identity and the wisdom of our reason (Bernauer, 1992, p. 42). Once the line between mental well-being and illness is blurred, it becomes possible to think differently about mental health. For instance, it may be more fruitful to think in terms of a spectrum along which varying degrees of well-being could be charted. This might encourage greater acknowledgement of fluctuating levels of mental well-being for many people at various times in the lifecycle. In this way, the mechanism through which those deemed mentally ill become classified as "other" could be undermined. This in itself has the potential to ameliorate the extent of problems faced by people. The diminishing of stigma also could open space for reconsidering the social meanings attributed to problematic mental experience.

Implicit in any blurring of the line between mental health and illness is the need to rethink what it might mean to live a normal life. This issue is touched on by White in relation to diagnostic labels. Adopting neither a for nor an against position, he believes it is important to honour the ways in which people experience such labels as enabling. For instance, they might challenge feelings of personal inadequacy often experienced by people unable to live in customary ways. Or they might reduce the stress of being subject to cultural expectations associated with "wellness". At the same time, he thinks it reflects sadly on our culture that exemption from dominant cultural identity prescriptions requires inhabiting a site of illness. In his view, it is possible to assist people to locate alternative cultural sites which do not entail this requirement. This often involves tracing personal histories of protest against the dominant culture. He has found that in this process diagnoses and the exemptions they carry increasingly become irrelevant (White, 1995, pp. 118–119). By enabling people to step outside commonly accepted, but ill-fitting, ways of thinking and living without understanding themselves primarily as ill, such a shift undermines the idea of there being only one way to live a "normal" life.

The realization that a socially imposed identity can be refused also can incite broader political activity. For the "Power to Our Journeys" group this realization has involved a campaign for social justice:

> It has been important for us to experience our work to reclaim our lives from the troublesome voices and visions as a struggle against injustice . . . As we explore together notions of justice, we develop greater clarity about the fact that we do not have to put up with our lives being spoken about in ways that reduce us, in pathologising and marginalising ways. And we become more effective in our challenges to these ways of speaking about our lives and the lives of others who experience troublesome voices and visions.
>
> (Brigitte *et al.*, 1997, p. 29)

This type of challenge has included speaking out publicly against unhelpful professional attitudes and practices. In this way, the group seeks to destabilize privileged mental health discourse and contribute to its reformulation along radically different lines (Brigitte *et al.*, 1997, pp. 29–30). What is this if not an attempt to alter "the discourse itself in the way that Foucault envisioned an 'insurrection of knowledges' might accomplish?" Far from being politically conservative, narrative therapeutic work has the potential to undermine dominant cultural discourses about normality and mental illness at both individual and community levels.

At the heart of Fish's argument is the belief that Foucault would see *any* form of therapy as still working through discourses (about "therapists", "clients", "families", etc.) that are immune to change by the individual intentions of therapists or those consulting them (Fish, 1993, p. 225). In the same vein, Jim Birch points to Deborah Luepnitz's concern about using Foucault's work to inform a therapeutic method when his philosophical stance posits therapies as inevitably oppressive (Birch, 1995, p. 225). Yet, as claimed earlier, it can be argued that Foucault is not so much anti-therapy as interested in investigating the power effects of taken-for-granted categories of illness or pathology, normality and abnormality. Given his view of the mutual entanglement of power and knowledge, such discourses inevitably yield power effects. An exposé of the contingent status of these categories of knowledge and their power effects opens space for the reformulation of social practices in this area. Thus Foucault aims to make it more problematic for those authorized by dominant discourses to continue to speak and act in familiar, taken-for-granted ways. This type of critique is echoed in narrative therapy's problematization of key therapeutic realities. Just as it is difficult, therefore, for those engaging with Foucault's work to emerge without a sense that certain commonplaces have been disturbed, many therapists engaging with narrative therapeutic ideas and practices are unlikely to conceive of themselves as therapists in previously characteristic ways. And this is precisely what Luepnitz identifies as an appropriate use of Foucault's work in the field of family therapy: "A Foucauldian 'impact' on family therapy would not have to do with practising different techniques, nor would it mean necessarily the end of practice. The point would be to understand ourselves differently as practitioners" (Luepnitz, 1992, p. 284). Yet notwithstanding Luepnitz's claim about not practising different techniques, when practitioners understand themselves differently the type of therapy they engage in also will be different. In the case of narrative therapy, this difference is in the direction of undermining therapy as a "system of obedience" to expert knowledge and given social structures.

OTHER INFLUENCES

While this chapter focuses primarily on the use of Foucault's thought in narrative therapy, it would be a mistake to see this as the only important influence. Despite inspiring much of its departure from therapeutic orthodoxy, Foucault has little to say about the positive role played by others in self-making and the gendered nature of existence. In relation to the former, Peta Bowden notes that Foucault's depiction of a relational notion of identity emphasizes the hierarchical and agonistic nature of our connections with others. The notions of struggle and resistance associated with these types of connections in Foucault's work lend an individualist tone to emancipatory practices of care for the self. Yet this narrows considerably the types of relationship which may enhance such practices:

> Because Foucault's understanding of the self cannot address inter-personal attachments such as intimate sharing, nurturing, spiritual solidarity or communal empowerment his view of care for the self misses the ethically significant ways in which engagement in these kinds of relations with other persons may contribute to one's caring relationship to oneself.
>
> (Bowden, 1992, p. 90)[6]

As outlined in Chapter 3, narrative therapy explicitly acknowledges the important role of others in strengthening revised identities. White's thinking in this area is inspired by the work of anthropologist Barbara Myerhoff. Central to Myerhoff's thought is the metaphor of "definitional ceremony" which "deal[s] with the problems of invisibility and margin-ality; [it is a] strateg[y] that provide[s] opportunities for being seen and in one's own terms, garnering witnesses to one's worth, vitality, and being" (Myerhoff, 1986, p. 267). In the therapeutic context, this type of validation occurs through the identification and recruitment of "outsider witnesses" whose presence helps to enrich the texture of the preferred stories that unfold in therapy, thereby rendering them more available for performance in concrete practices of thinking and living. Chapter 3 described this process in relation to "re-membering" practices and reflecting teamwork.

ASCENDING NOTIONS OF POWER

While a focus on others' contribution to self-making signals a departure from Foucault, nonetheless it is possible to draw a parallel between the notion of power implicit in his later work and reflecting teamwork. The type of self-making advocated by Foucault as a practice of freedom entails an ascending rather than hierarchical, top-down notion of power. This emanates from the micro-level of the individual or group working its way outward and upward to affect given relations of power at the local and more macro levels. In reflecting teamwork, an ascending notion of power is evident in the incorporation of structures and processes which decentre therapists and privilege people's knowledge about their experience of problems and the shape of preferred narratives. It is reflected further in acknowledgement of the powerful effects of this work on team members and through a demystification of the workings of the therapy itself (see White, 1995, pp. 172–198; 1999, pp. 52–82).

THE FEMINIST INFLUENCE

A claim for the significance of others in self-making projects easily blends into a discussion of the influence of feminist thought on narrative therapy. Feminists have long been aware of the importance of solidarity among women in the struggle against imposed identities. A further parallel between narrative therapy and feminism can be seen in the former's privileging of the understandings of those attending therapy and the feminist claim that "every woman is the authority over her own experience" (Hare-Mustin and Marecek, 1994, p. 16). There is also the politicizing of the personal in feminist thought and narrative therapy's emphasis on the link between selfhood and the broader sociopolitical context. These and other similarities probably reflect the influence of feminist ideas on the development of narrative therapy (see White, 1995, p. 12; 2001). One area where this clearly is the case is in regard to gender power relations. While this type of feminist analysis permeates the approach generally, it is evident particularly in work with survivors (see Mann and Russell, 2002) and perpetrators of domestic violence and child sexual abuse. This work reflects an awareness of interpersonal relationship politics and the broader patriarchal context within which violence and abuse take place. Such an orientation enables a challenge to common practices of pathologizing violence and abuse survivors, obscuring the responsibility of perpetrators and ignoring the link between dominant cultural beliefs and impoverished self and relationship narratives. It also points to the need for accountability practices when male therapists work with female survivors and male perpetrators of violence and abuse (White, 1995, pp. 82–111, 155–171).[7]

EXTENDING FOUCAULT'S THOUGHT

Narrative therapy's emphasis on the important role played by others in re-authoring projects and its adoption of a feminist analysis of gender relations clearly distinguish it from Foucault's thought. Nonetheless, this does not signal irreconcilable differences. In terms of the role of others, Foucault's notion of relational selfhood highlights the way in which assigned identities are constituted socially and historically. While this type of understanding is an important precursor to the idea of emancipatory projects, as noted an emphasis on the intersubjective nature of identity processes is less evident in his work on self-fashioning. In this regard, narrative therapy's emphasis on the positive significance of others can be seen to supplement Foucault's analysis of the disempowering dimension of intersubjectivity. By building on and extending this aspect of his thought, greater scope is provided for the application of Foucauldian ideas in re-authoring projects.

The issue of gender constitutes a further blindspot in Foucault's thought. Regardless of the motivation behind this,[8] it limits the usefulness of both deconstructive and reconstructive aspects of his thought. A number of feminists sympathetic to the general thrust of his work have attempted to correct such an omission through the incorporation of gender analyses.[9] In a similar vein, narrative therapy's recognition of the significance of gender cuts across this problem. Yet once again rather than indicating a radical departure from Foucault, the incorporation of a gender analysis helps operationalize more fully his aim of encouraging people to refuse their assigned identities.

SUMMARY

Although the use of Foucault's work in the therapeutic domain may appear paradoxical, I argue that it need not be. I have attempted to demonstrate the ways in which, in the case of narrative therapy, the application of these ideas remains within the spirit of Foucault's endeavours. This is reflected in its destabilization of key therapeutic assumptions at the heart of which lies a notion of objective and universal reason. Foucault's view that all knowledge is enmeshed in relations of power provides a rationale for investigating the power effects of such assumptions. Moreover, his notion of the productive force of power highlights the crucial issue of the self's relation to broader structures of power. Of particular significance is the repudiation of any notion of a "deep" or "true" self. It was argued that this aligns narrative therapy more closely with Foucault's thought than with the psychoanalytic version of selfhood he targets. Viewed in this light, this approach can be seen as an instance of the claim that the very power relations that constrain people also can provide the possibility for a creative self-expression. Thus just as the therapeutic domain can perpetuate oppressive power practices, it also can provide a site of subversion to such practices. In relation to emancipatory projects, narrative therapy applies Foucault's general point to particular, individual cases as reflected in its practical investigation of the historical processes that have constituted individuals as they are, and the exploration of possibilities for self-making more in line with their preferred ways of being. The forging of re-authored identities in relation to the sociohistorical context frees people from subjection to an essential identity and leaves open the possibility of ongoing self-making. In this way narrative therapy can be seen to echo Foucault's aim

> to show people that they are much freer than they feel, that people accept as truth, as evidence, some themes which have been built

up at a certain moment during history, and that this so-called evidence can be criticized and destroyed.

(R. Martin, 1988, p. 10)

The discussion of narrative therapy's use of Foucault was concluded by engagement with two strands of critique from within the family therapy literature. In the final section of the chapter, I pointed to the important contributions of cultural anthropology and feminist thought on the development of narrative therapy. In the same way that feminists sympathetic to the general tenor of Foucault's thought have sought to extend his analysis by incorporating a focus on gender, it was argued that narrative therapy does likewise in relation to the positive significance of others in identity revision and with regard to gender power relations. This points to a further parallel between certain strands of feminist thought and narrative therapy.

CONCLUSION

This book has focused on the relationship women have with themselves. It depicts self-policing as a common feature of this relationship. Identified by Michel Foucault as a key mechanism of modern social control, self-policing tends to give rise to a strict overseer type of relation to the self which precludes spontaneity and keeps individuals tied to prescribed identities. In illuminating the sociopolitical dimension of this type of internal practice, Foucault's analysis challenges a common belief in its inevitable status while also providing acknowledgement of the stakes involved in transformative efforts. At the same time, his relentless emphasis on the contingent rather than necessary nature of modern identities inspires such efforts. While he does not investigate the relationship between gender and self-policing, I have argued that factors such as the legacy of subordinate status and a frequent imbalance between care for others and care for the self render women vulnerable to heightened self-policing. This can entail intensified surveillance and judgement of the self, unfavourable comparisons with others, various punishments of the body, mind and spirit and personal isolation. Self-policing can operate in relation to a wide range of areas including self and body image, sexuality, intimate relations, mothering, friendship, study and career performance, and so on. To speak generally of such a practice in women's lives, however, is not to imply a uniformity of experience. While the category of gender can illuminate certain common themes, once other factors are considered a multiplicity of intersecting influences may affect the relative intensity of self-policing. If this practice ensures the measuring of self-worth in terms of conformity to accepted norms, the strength of the "inner gaze" is likely to vary according to women's relationship to broad social categories of race, class, sexuality, health, and so forth, and to experiences of violence and abuse. This does not deny the possibility of intra-group difference. For individual women, too, self-policing may exert more of a hold in relation to certain aspects of life or at different times in the lifecycle.

Because self-policing has become such a commonplace part of the psychic make up of individuals, it is difficult to subject it to critical scrutiny. I described a therapeutic approach capable of undermining its apparent inevitability and of exploring the social context in which it prospers. Narrative therapy's awareness of the link between identity processes and broader structures of power leads to the development of practices which assist people to challenge ways of thinking and living that have come to oppress them. One example of the latter is the internalizing discourse of modern western societies which encourages a sense of personal deficiency when problems emerge. As a counter to the unhelpful, at times unjust, effects of such a discourse externalizing conversations help people begin to separate themselves from problematic experience and to gain a sense of agency in relation to it. This type of conversation also facilitates exploration of the broader context in which problems arise, thereby highlighting the relationship between personal struggles and commonly accepted ideas and practices. From this position, a revision of people's relationship with problems becomes possible. Nonetheless, Johnella Bird points to the way in which an emphasis on the problem and the person being separate tends to reinforce the very idea of self-regulated identity opposed by narrative therapy. It was argued that her alternative notion of "relational externalizing" offers an effective way of embodying relational identity, thereby undermining belief in the intrinsic nature of self-policing. Once this occurs, negotiating different ways of relating to the self becomes possible. This process can be facilitated by identifying individual (and family) histories of resistance to oppressive identity practices. This inspires ongoing acts of resistance and provides information about women's preferred ways of being with themselves. In revising the relationship with self-policing, the relational aspect of preferred attributes or feeling states continues to be emphasized. This allows acknowledgement of women's active participation in enacting these while diminishing the power of self-policing when they are underperformed. In turn, this encourages exploration of the context in which preferred attributes are more likely to thrive. Revised identity practices are made more available for performance in day-to-day life through their legitimation and enrichment by supportive others.

In further reflection on strategies likely to undermine women's self-policing, I discussed the idea of greater care for the self. This discussion drew on aspects of Foucault's later work which posit the relationship one has with oneself as an important component of ethics. Such a notion implicitly challenges the imbalance in many women's lives between care for others and care for the self which can heighten vulnerability to living by the expectations of others. The type of care for the self advocated by Foucault involves creative interaction with given relations of power in order to actively participate in the fashioning of different subjectivities. It was argued, however, that the ancient notion of self-mastery on which he draws is unlikely to facilitate this. I suggested instead the potential of bell hooks' notion of structuring relationships around the principle of love and

Maria Lugones' non-imperialistic approach. Specifically, I advocated the value of friendship as an organizing principle in women's self-relations. One way of facilitating this in the therapeutic context is through the practice of relating to the self as one would to a friend. This can undermine the strict overseer type of relationship characteristic of self-policing, thereby increasing access to the care and compassion so often extended to others. Interestingly, the greater level of self-acceptance associated with friendship with the self tends to enhance possibilities for desired change. Emphasis was placed on the political nature of work on the self which seeks to disturb unwanted ways of relating to and understanding the self.

Narrative therapy is inspired significantly by Foucault's thought. While this may strike some readers as paradoxical, I argued that this approach remains true to the spirit of Foucault's endeavours. This is reflected in its investigation of the specific forms of knowledge and relations of power operating in the therapeutic realm. Moreover, the refusal to situate its practices within discourses of human nature places narrative therapy closer to Foucault than the type of confessional practices he criticizes. Both deconstructive and re-authoring work echo his view that identity practices do not have to be informed by scientific knowledge, and that an historically contingent notion of subjectivity provides greater scope for human creativity and freedom. In narrative therapy, it is claimed that rejection of the objective truth claims of psychological discourse increases, rather than decreases, the moral responsibility of therapists in relation to the real effects of specific practices. Taking responsibility for the concrete effects of interactions with those seeking assistance and a concern for the socially marginalized are two instances of narrative therapy taking a clear moral stance.

Other important influences on narrative therapy include cultural anthropology and feminism. The former inspires an emphasis on the positive role played by others in the renegotiation of identity. In relation to feminist thought, its influence is evident in the incorporation of an analysis of gender power relations.

SOME FINAL REFLECTIONS

Just as no single narrative is able to capture the full complexity of lived experience, any theoretical or practical analysis is unlikely to offer a fully comprehensive account of its subject matter. Human experience is too rich, messy, and multi-dimensional to be subsumed within a singular set of ideas. The aim of this book is not to set in concrete certain ideas about women's self-surveillance but rather to increase the visibility of such a practice in order to render it more available for ongoing reflection, debate and transformation. This does not negate the fact that negative attitudes towards the self provide a focal point for a range of feminist therapies. Feminists have long been aware of the destructive impact of feelings of unworthiness, self-doubt, self-criticism, self-hate, and so forth on women's sense of self. Nonetheless, the tenacious and insidious ways in which self-policing practices can continue to tyrannize or limit women's lives warrants ongoing illumination. An exploration of such practices can form part of therapy in relation to a wide range of experiences. These include relationship and parenting practices, eating disorders, violence and abuse, depression, rape, sexuality, grief, workplace relations, ill health and so on.[1] When the presence of self-surveillance/judgement/self-criticism/insidious comparisons with others/personal exile is identified and its impact explored, it becomes possible to investigate the ways in which such practices interweave with, and frequently intensify, the particular concerns or problems which bring women to therapy. As such, this type of enquiry offers a way of unpacking the often multi-layered character of problematic experience while simultaneously providing an important avenue for change.

In this account, I have focused on the sociopolitical dimension of self-policing because of the need in strongly individualistic societies to expose over and over again the existence of social forces which fashion individual identity and experience. As I have argued, rather than diminishing individual agency and responsibility, an understanding of context can increase possibilities for active intervention in one's life. Other reflections on women's self-policing might focus on different factors. For instance, some readers may want to see a role for the unconscious. Although a number of commentators have pointed to the social construction rather than given nature of such an entity (see Burr, 1995, p. 127; 2003), Jane Flax (and others) see an important role for notions of the unconscious in efforts to better understand human complexity and ambivalence. While deeply critical of many aspects of traditional psychoanalysis, Flax nonetheless points to subversive elements. In particular, the depiction of a partially independent internal world permeated by desire and fantasy, which is capable of unconsciously affecting thought, is seen as disturbing the notion of a unitary stable self, autonomous reason and the equation of consciousness with mind. This corresponds with a postmodern understanding that we inhabit a plurality of selves, some of which are inconsistent (Flax, 1993, pp. 136–138). I also have referred to the work of feminist object relations therapists for whom unconscious processes reflect existing child-rearing and gender social arrangements. Some attempts have been made to bridge a discourse/power networks approach within critical psychology and certain feminist reworkings of psychoanalytic theory. This is seen to provide a link with "the many complex and often contradictory fragments of past experience which lie beyond everyday consciousness" (Henwood, 1995, p. 503) and impinge on the present. The critical issue in relation to these and other approaches (including the one I advocate) is not whether they are true or false in an objective sense, but rather how useful they prove in explicating and helping to transform unwanted self-policing. From the perspective of this book, those approaches most likely to accomplish this will emphasize the idea of relational identity. This challenges the inevitability of self-policing and acknowledges the diverse and complex ways in which women's selves are constituted through interaction with a range of sociohistorical forces.

Finally, the discussion of self-policing unfolding throughout this book derives from the therapeutic context. While such a context can, and frequently does, depoliticize women's experience, I have pointed to the subversive potential of certain types of therapy. Further potential for radicalizing the therapeutic project lies in the broader applicability of its knowledges. For the present purposes, the understandings gained from an interplay between women's concrete experiences and theoretical reflections in therapy can provide the basis for identifying, and trying to better understand the impact of, gendered self-policing in a variety of social contexts. For instance, how does this relationship get played out in the classroom at various levels of education? What might a focus on self-policing and gender issues contribute to reflection on socialization practices, eating disorder programmes, social work perspectives, debate on media representations of gender, police domestic violence training, and more generally to theories of selfhood which provide the basis for a range of social policies and perspectives. By drawing on knowledge negotiated in the therapeutic environment, a broader investigation of gendered self-policing could significantly enhance possibilities for transforming this practice of power.

126

NOTES

Introduction

1. Thanks to Peta Bowden for these points.
2. This and other aspects of Bird's work are elaborated in Chapter 4.

1 A lens for viewing self-policing

1. For a summary of other similarities see Sawicki (1998, pp. 93–94).

2 Gender and self-policing

1. See Jordan *et al.* (1991).
2. A focus on women's nurturing role is not intended to depict men as uncaring. Men's care, for example, traditionally has entailed financial provision for and protection of families. Nonetheless, many working-class women have shared financial responsibility while continuing to be the primary emotional and physical nurturers. In recent decades, the expectation of joint responsibility for financial provision for families has extended to middle-class women. There also has been an increasing expectation for women to assume greater self-responsibility. Finally, there is the issue of men's common association of care with problem-solving rather than nurturance. (A further reference to this point is made in Chapter 5, Note 6.)
3. Such a notion builds on the early work of authors such as Carol Gilligan (see 1982) and Nel Noddings (see 1984).
4. Offering an alternative understanding of relationship, Homiak describes Aristotle's model of virtuous citizenship. Central to this model is an understanding that contributing to the good of others includes doing things that will nurture and sustain their feelings of self-love and that at times this might *not* take the form of satisfying their wants (Homiak, 1993, p. 15).
5. See Jordan *et al.* (1991, p. 112).
6. In relation to documentation of decades of mother-blaming in the clinical literature of the 1960s, 1970s and into the 1980s regarding the sexual abuse of children by fathers see Dwyer and Miller (1996, p. 139).
7. While White is referring specifically to the type of self-policing common to sufferers of eating disorders, these descriptions capture a range of practices characteristic, to varying degrees, of many women's self-relationship.

8. This is an insight central to the work of some of the early second wave feminists (for example, see MacKinnon, 1989, pp. 95, 100).
9. See Lorde (1983, 1984); hooks (1981); Smith (1982); Lugones (1991); Lugones and Spelman (1990); We Appear Silent to People Who are Deaf to What We Say (1989).
10. Thus difference can provide an exit point to the self-policing of dominant identity prescriptions. This is reflected further in a study of adolescent females in which African Americans were much less susceptible than their white counterparts to dominant notions of beauty, body image and weight. For African American girls, the idea of developing one's own style in line with given physical endowments and one's social and economic milieu was preferred over conformity to a uniform standard (Parker *et al.*, 1995, pp. 103–114). (Thanks to Diana Tietjens Meyers for pointing me to this study.)
11. Thanks to Sharon Gollan for this point.
12. As in the case of groups marginalized by the dominant culture, many women living in situations of domestic violence are forced to intensify surveillance of their behaviour in order to try to minimize levels of violence against them and their children. This also can be the case for children subject to sexual abuse in the home environment (Bell, 1993, p. 65).
13. This process is elaborated in Chapters 3 and 4.
14. See Ward (1984, pp. 196–197).

3 Challenging negative identity practices – narrative therapy

1. For the views of a number of feminist practitioners on points of convergence between feminism and the ideas and practices embodied in this approach, see Russell and Carey (2003, pp. 67–91). Nonetheless, advocating its usefulness is not intended to preclude other possible feminist frameworks. Nor is it meant to suggest that narrative therapy is exclusively concerned with women's oppression.
2. See White (1995, pp. 68–69). In relation to both this practice and that of generally inviting feedback on the effects of the therapy, Leela Anderson highlights the problem of simply assuming this reciprocal sharing or direct request will create the necessary psychological space for people to speak frankly. As she notes, such an assumption masks the complexities involved in the power relations and what genuinely supports any client, especially disenfranchised persons, being able to privilege their own experience. These complexities are likely to be increased in the case of women consulting male therapists. She suggests that the challenge for therapists is to carry the knowledge that professional position, gender, class, sexuality, and so forth, are interwoven into the fabric of all conversation and have ongoing effects despite accountability efforts (Leela Anderson, personal communication, October 2000).
3. For a fuller account of these processes see White (1995, pp. 155–171; 1991); Jenkins (1990).
4. Despite the emphasis on people's relationship to problems, concern has been expressed about the way in which the idea of separation between the person and their problem inadvertently reinforces the dominant idea of self-contained identity. This concern is taken up in Chapter 4's discussion of immanent critiques of narrative therapy.
5. He argues that while the views of critical psychologists are tied to the sociohistorical context, it is nonetheless possible to mount a more ethically

defensible position than those they critique. Such a position is grounded in the recognition of objectively existing patterns of domination which give rise to the exploitation and oppression of certain individuals and groups (Parker, 1997, pp. 295–297).

6. For a recent discussion of aspects of this issue in the narrative therapy literature, see Madigan (2003).

4 Immanent critiques: expanded possibilities for refusing self-policing

1. For an account of similarities between the systemic family therapy approach and narrative therapy, see Flaskas et al. (2000, pp. 126–128).

2. A similar notion is expressed by Chenoweth et al. who point to the need to take into account an understanding of the biological changes resulting from abuse, trauma, neglect, etc. (Chenoweth et al., 1997, p. 223).

3. For a very readable account of these ideas see Burr (1995, 2003); see also Parker and Shotter (1990); Parker (1999b); Gergen (1999, 2001).

4. For an account of the way in which subjectivity is constituted relationally in heterosexual relationships, see Holloway (1989).

5. An understanding of the meaning of attributes identified as desirable needs to be negotiated rather than assumed. For instance, confidence may mean different things to different women – some women may want to define it in a way that precludes arrogance and others will construe it in other ways.

6. Clear parallels exist between the type of therapeutic approach outlined and the feminist practice of consciousness raising. Most obvious is the contextualization of individual women's lives within a sociopolitical framework. This assists the move away from a sense of personal deficit or inadequacy and undermines the common experience of isolation. The therapeutic environment described offers specific strategies for diminishing or overturning entrenched aspects of self-policing and associated identity prescriptions and for the performance of preferred identities. The former can continue to dominate women's lives despite a clear intellectual commitment to self-remaking. There is also the charting of a history that stands beyond impoverished self-understandings. Moreover, the renegotiation of identity does not involve the search for universally authentic ways of being. Finally, this type of therapy has the potential to facilitate the politicization of many women whom feminism may not otherwise reach. On this final point see Swan (1999, pp. 111, 113–114).

7. Although I refer to the occurrence of such moments within the therapeutic context these, of course, are not restricted to such a context.

8. One therapist recounts a woman's description of her self-orientation as having been "like a lion tamer with a bullwhip" compared to an attentive, understanding attitude towards others (Jordan et al., 1991, p. 78).

9. For further examples see Cherubin et al. (1998, pp. 16–17) and Silent Too Long (1998a, 1998b).

5 An ethics of care for the self

1. McNay's critique of these (and other) aspects of Foucault's later work has been contested by some feminists (for example see Lloyd, 1996, pp. 241–264 and Sawicki, 1998, pp. 93–107). In relation to debate about whether Foucault's

notion of care for the self is derived from the "virile mastery" model of the ancient Greeks, see Vintges (2004).

2. The often limited nature of women's care for others is referred to later.

3. This is not to deny that some women engage in violent behaviour towards others, including children and other women.

4. For some women, however, self-harming behaviours may not be connected to an impoverished self-narrative but rather can be life strategies, albeit limited and costly ones, for dealing with the threat of overwhelming emotions or memories.

5. It is not intended to imply that this is the only way of facilitating friendship with the self. Rather it is suggested that given many women's training in care for others, this offers one entry point.

6. Nonetheless, as noted earlier, many working- (and increasingly middle-) class women have contributed to the economic viability of the family. The male protector role also has diminished with the increase in female-headed house-holds and the greater independence of many women. Generally, these changes tend not to have led to men taking over or sharing women's physical and emotional nurturing roles. Increasing awareness of the unequal distribution of women's caring responsibilities has given rise to greater involvement by some men in emotional nurturance. While this is encouraging both on egalitarian grounds and because it provides greater opportunities for the expansion of men's emotional capacities and greater care for women, it is still quite common to hear women describe an imbalance in the emotional energy invested in family relationships despite the fact that their male partners are generally caring. This may, in part, be due to men commonly associating care with problem-solving rather than emotional support and availability (for instance see Tannen, 1991, pp. 49–53). Some heterosexual women also describe continuing to feel unsupported by their partners in many of the less obvious practical tasks required for familial well-being – for example thinking ahead and organizing various tasks that contribute to less domestic stress and create more time for relaxed interaction.

6 Foucault and therapy – a contradiction?

1. For a recent account of the use of Foucault's thought within this approach, see White (2002).

2. In 1990 research highlighted the considerable deprivation usually experienced by recipients of the lowest 30 per cent of income levels in most western societies. This could include poor housing, unemployment and lack of access to adequate food, clothing and/or health care. Women, non-dominant cultural groups, the unemployed or working poor usually comprise a disproportionate amount of this 30 per cent compared to their numbers in the population as a whole. Waldegrave points to various studies which demonstrate the frequently adverse consequences of such deprivations on people's psychological and physical health (Waldegrave, 1990, pp. 21–23).

3. See White (1997, pp. 217–218; 2002).

4. See for example Jane Flax's postmodern and feminist critique which challenges the type of identity categories and standards of normalcy and health generated and maintained, in part, by psychoanalytic discourse (Flax, 1993, pp. 37–58; also see Henriques et al., 1998).

5. For a commentary on the use of power in White's work see Tomm (1993, pp. 62–80).

6. See McNay (1994, p. 152).
7. For an account of the incorporation of both gender and culture accountability, see Tamasese and Waldegrave (1993).
8. Some commentators on the later work see the neglect of gender issues as consistent with attempts to think in terms other than the dichotomies of masculine and feminine (see McNay, 1992, p. 194).
9. For instance see Bartky (1988, pp. 61–86; 1998, pp. 15–27); Bordo (1989, pp. 13–33); Sawicki (1986, pp. 23–36; 1988, pp. 177–191; 1991); Morris (1988, pp. 21–42); B. Martin (1988, pp. 3–19); Butler (1986, pp. 505–516).

Conclusion

1. Nonetheless, the possibility of negative self-policing *not* being a feature of some women's self-relationship also must be held in mind.

BIBLIOGRAPHY

Allen, B. (1998). Foucault and Modern Political Philosophy. In J. Moss (ed.), *The Later Foucault: Politics and Philosophy*. London: Sage Publications, 164–198.

Bartky, S.L. (1988). Foucault, Femininity, and the Modernization of Patriarchal Power. In I. Diamond and L. Quinby (eds), *Feminism and Foucault: Reflections on Resistance*. Boston: Northeastern University Press, 61–86.

Bartky, S.L. (1990). *Femininity and Domination: Studies in the Phenomenology of Oppression*. New York & London: Routledge.

Bartky, S.L. (1998). Skin Deep: Femininity as a Disciplinary Regime. In B.-A. Bar On and A. Ferguson (eds), *Daring to be Good: Essays in Feminist Ethico-Politics*. New York & London: Routledge, 15–27.

Beaudoin, M.-N. (1999). Silencing Critical Voices: An Internet Journal. Retrieved 13 January, 2004 from http://www.voices.com/issue2.html, 1–3.

Bell, V. (1993). *Interrogating Incest: Feminism, Foucault and the Law*. London & New York: Routledge.

Bernauer, J. (1992). *Michel Foucault's Force of Flight: Toward an Ethics for Thought*. New Jersey: Humanities Press.

Birch, J. (1995). Chasing the Rainbow's End, and Why it Matters: A Coda to Pocock, Frosh and Larner. *Journal of Family Therapy* (Vol. 17 No. 2) 219–228.

Bird, J. (1993). Family Therapy . . . What's in a Name? *Australian and New Zealand Journal of Family Therapy* (Vol. 14 No. 2) 81–84.

Bird, J. (February 1999). Issues of Gender in Therapy. Paper presented at *Narrative Therapy and Community Work Conference*, University of Adelaide, South Australia.

Bird, J. (2000). *The Heart's Narrative: Therapy and Navigating Life's Contradictions*. Auckland, New Zealand: Edge Press.

Bordo, S. (1989). The Body and the Reproduction of Femininity: A Feminist Appropriation of Foucault. In A. Jaggar and S. Bordo (eds), *Gender/Body/Knowledge: Feminist Reconstructions of Being and Knowing*. New Brunswick, NJ: Rutgers University Press, 13–33.

Bordo, S. (1990). Feminism, Postmodernism, and Gender-Scepticism. In L.J. Nicholson (ed.), *Feminism/Postmodernism*. New York: Routledge, 133–156.

Bowden, P. (1992). *Caring: An Investigation in Gender-Sensitive Ethics*. PhD dissertation, Department of Philosophy, McGill University, Montréal, Canada.

132

Bowden, P. (1997). *Caring: Gender-Sensitive Ethics*. London & New York: Routledge.

Brigitte, Sue, Mem and Veronika (1997). Power to Our Journeys: Companions on a Journey. *Dulwich Centre Newsletter* (No. 1) 25–33.

Bubenzer, D., West, J. and Boughner, S. (1994). Interview with Michael White and the Narrative Perspective in Therapy. *The Family Journal: Counselling and Therapy for Couples and Families* (Vol. 2 No. 1) 71–83.

Burr, V. (1995). *An Introduction to Social Constructionism*. London: Routledge.

Burr, V. (2003). *Social Constructionism*. London: Routledge.

Butler, J. (January 1986). Variations on Sex and Gender: Beauvoir, Wittig, and Foucault. *Praxis International* (Vol. 5 No. 4) 505–516.

Butler, J. (1990a). *Gender Trouble: Feminism and the Subversion of Identity*. New York: Routledge.

Butler, J. (1990b). Gender Trouble, Feminist Theory, and Psychoanalytic Discourse. In L.J. Nicholson (ed.), *Feminism/Postmodernism*. New York: Routledge, 324–340.

Caplan, P. and Hall-McCorquodale, I. (1985). Mother-Blaming in Major Clinical Journals. *American Journal of Orthopsychiatry* (Vol. 55 No. 3) 345–353.

Chenoweth, B., Roth, J., Stark, A. and Wills, A. (1997). Beyond Narrative. *Australian and New Zealand Journal of Family Therapy* (Vol. 18 No. 4) 222–225.

Cherubin, M., Flynn, W. and Morgan, A. (1998). Towards Power and Change: Working with Women Carers within the Mental Health System. *Gecko: A Journal of Deconstruction and Narrative Ideas in Therapeutic Practice* (Vol. 2) 7–22.

A Conversation with Kiwi Tamasese and Charles Waldegrave: Power and Politics in Practice. (1994). *Dulwich Centre Newsletter* (No. 1) pp. 20–27.

Darier, E. (July 1996). Michel Foucault's Contribution to Environmental Ethics: Environmental Resistance and the Construction of a Green Self. *Working Paper Series 96–6*, Environmental Policy Unit, School of Policy Studies, Queens University, Kingston, Ontario, Canada, 1–18.

Dickerson, V. (1998). Silencing Critical Voices: An Interview with Marie-Nathalie Beaudoin. *Gecko: A Journal of Deconstruction and Narrative Ideas in Therapeutic Practice* (Vol. 2) 29–45.

Dickerson, V., Zimmerman, J. and Berndt, L. (1994). Challenging Developmental Truths – Separating from Separation. *Dulwich Centre Newsletter* (No. 4) 2–12.

Doan, R. (Fall 1998). The King is Dead; Long Live the King: Narrative Therapy and Practicing What We Preach. *Family Process* (Vol. 37 No. 3) 379–385.

Dwyer, J. and Miller, R. (1996). Disenfranchised Grief after Incest: The Experience of Victims/Daughters, Mothers/Wives. *Australian and New Zealand Journal of Family Therapy* (Vol. 17 No. 3) 137–145.

Eichenbaum, L. and Orbach, S. (1985). *Understanding Women: A New Expanded Version of Outside In . . . Inside Out*. Harmondsworth: Penguin.

Elliott, H. (1998). En-gendering Distinctions: Postmodernism, Feminism, and Narrative Therapy. In S. Madigan and I. Law (eds), *Praxis: Situating Discourse, Feminism and Politics in Narrative Therapies*. Vancouver, Canada: The Cardigan Press, 35–61.

Epston, D. and White, M. (1990). Consulting your Consultants: The

Documentation of Alternative Knowledges. *Dulwich Centre Newsletter* (No. 4) 25–35.

Fish, V. (1993). Poststructuralism in Family Therapy: Interrogating the Narrative/ Conversational Mode. *Journal of Marital and Family Therapy* (Vol. 19 No. 3) 221–232.

Flaskas, C. *et al.* (2000). Dialogues of Diversity in Therapy: A Virtual Symposium. *Australian and New Zealand Journal of Family Therapy* (Vol. 21 No. 3) 121–143.

Flax, J. (1993). *Disputed Subjects: Essays on Psychoanalysis, Politics and Philosophy*. New York & London: Routledge.

Foucault, M. (1967). *Madness and Civilisation: A History of Insanity in the Age of Reason*. London: Tavistock.

Foucault, M. (1973). *The Birth of the Clinic: An Archaeology of Medical Perception*. London: Tavistock.

Foucault, M. (1978). *The History of Sexuality: Volume 1 An Introduction*. New York & London: Penguin.

Foucault, M. (1979). *Discipline and Punish: The Birth of the Prison*. Harmondsworth: Penguin.

Foucault, M. (1982). The Subject and Power. Afterword. In H.L. Dreyfus and P. Rabinow, *Michel Foucault: Beyond Structuralism and Hermeneutics*. Chicago: University of Chicago Press, 208–226.

Foucault, M. (1986). *The Use of Pleasure: Volume Two of the History of Sexuality*, New York: Vintage Books.

Foucault, M. (1988). The Ethic of Care for the Self as a Practice of Freedom: An Interview with Michel Foucault on January 20, 1984. In J. Bernauer and D. Rasmussen (eds), *The Final Foucault*. Cambridge, MA: MIT Press, 1–20.

Foucault, M. (1990). *The Care of the Self: The History of Sexuality Volume 3*. London: Penguin.

Foucault, M. (1991). Questions of Method. In G. Burchell, C. Gordon and P. Miller (eds), *The Foucault Effect: Studies in Governmentality*. Chicago: University of Chicago Press, 73–86.

Fraser, N. (1989). *Unruly Practices: Power, Discourse, and Gender in Contemporary Social Theory*. Minneapolis: University of Minnesota Press.

Freedman, J. and Combs, G. (1996). *Narrative Therapy: The Social Construction of Preferred Realities*. New York: W.W. Norton.

Freer, M. (1997). Taking a Defiant Stand against Sexual Abuse and the Mother-Blaming Discourse. *Gecko: A Journal of Deconstruction and Narrative Ideas in Therapeutic Practice* (Vol. 1) 5–28.

Gergen, K. (1999). *An Invitation to Social Construction*. London: Sage.

Gergen, K. (2001). *Social Construction in Context*. London: Sage.

Gilligan, C. (1982). *In a Different Voice: Psychological Theory and Women's Development*. Cambridge, MA: Harvard University Press.

Gordon, C. (ed.) (1980). *Power/Knowledge: Selected Interviews and Other Writings, 1972–1977*. Brighton: Harvester.

Grimshaw, J. (1986). *Feminist Philosophers: Women's Perspectives on Philosophical Traditions*. Brighton, Sussex: Wheatsheaf Books Ltd.

Hare-Mustin, R. (March 1994). Discourses in the Mirrored Room: A Postmodern Analysis of Therapy. *Family Process* (Vol. 33 No. 1) 19–35.

Hare-Mustin, R. and Marecek, J. (1994). Feminism and Postmodernism: Dilemmas and Points of Resistance. *Dulwich Centre Newsletter* (No. 4) 13–19.

Hart, B. (1995). Re-authoring the Stories We Work By: Situating the Narrative Approach in the Presence of the Family of Therapists. *Australian and New Zealand Journal of Family Therapy* (Vol. 16 No. 4) 181–189.

Henriques, J., Holloway, W., Urwin, C., Venn, C. and Walkerdine, V. (1998). *Changing the Subject: Psychology, Social Regulation and Subjectivity*. London & New York: Routledge.

Henwood, K.L. (1995). Adult Mother–Daughter Relationships: Subjectivity, Power and Critical Psychology. *Theory and Psychology* (Vol. 5 No. 4) 483–510.

Holloway, W. (1989). *Subjectivity and Method in Psychology: Gender, Meaning and Science*. London: Sage Publications.

Homiak, M. (1993). Feminism and Aristotle's Rational Ideal. In L.M. Antony and C. Witt (eds), *A Mind of One's Own: Feminist Essays on Reason and Objectivity*. Boulder, CO: Westview Press, 1–17.

hooks, b. (1981). *Ain't I a Woman? Black Women and Feminism*. Boston, MA: South End Press.

hooks, b. (1996). *Killing Rage: Ending Racism*. Harmondsworth: Penguin.

Houston, B. (1989). Prolegomena to Future Caring. In M.M. Brabeck (ed.), *Who Cares? Theory, Research, and Educational Implications of the Ethic of Care*. New York: Praeger, 84–100.

Hoy, D.C. (1998). Foucault and Critical Theory. In J. Moss (ed.), *The Later Foucault: Politics and Philosophy*. London: Sage Publications, 18–32.

Jenkins, A. (1990). *Invitations to Responsibility: The Therapeutic Engagement of Men who are Violent and Abusive*. South Australia: Dulwich Centre Publications.

Jenkins, A. (1994). Therapy for Abuse or Therapy as Abuse: Power and Politics in Practice. *Dulwich Centre Newsletter* (No. 1) 11–19.

Jordan, J., Kaplan, A., Baker Miller, J., Stiver, I. and Surrey, J. (1991). *Women's Growth in Connection: Writings from the Stone Center*. New York: The Guilford Press.

Kamsler, A. (1990). Her-Story in the Making: Therapy with Women who were Sexually Abused in Childhood. In M. Durrant and C. White (eds), *Ideas for Therapy with Sexual Abuse*. South Australia: Dulwich Centre Publications, 9–36.

Kritzman, L.D. (ed.) (1988). *Michel Foucault: Politics, Philosophy, Culture – Interviews and Other Writings 1977–1984*. New York: Routledge.

Laird, J. (1994). Changing Women's Narratives: Taking Back the Discourse. In L.V. Davis (ed.), *Building on Women's Strengths: A Social Work Agenda for the Twenty-First Century*. New York: The Haworth Press, 179–210.

Law, I. (1998a). Attention Deficit Disorders: Therapy with a Shoddily Built Construct. In S. Madigan and I. Law (eds), *Praxis: Situating Discourse, Feminism and Politics in Narrative Therapies*. Vancouver, Canada: The Cardigan Press, 109–140.

Law, I. (1998b). Problem Gambling and Therapy: Exploring Alternative Metaphors to "Addiction". In S. Madigan and I. Law (eds), *Praxis: Situating Discourse, Feminism and Politics in Narrative Therapies*. Vancouver, Canada: The Cardigan Press, 163–194.

Law, I. and Madigan, S. (1994). Introduction: Power and Politics in Practice. *Dulwich Centre Newsletter* (No. 1) 3–6.

Law, I. and Madigan, S. (1998). Discourse Not Language: The Shift from a Modernist View of Language to a Post-Structural Analysis of Discourse in Family Therapy. In S. Madigan and I. Law (eds), *Praxis: Situating Discourse, Feminism and Politics in Narrative Therapies*. Vancouver, Canada: The Cardigan Press, 1–12.

Lloyd, M. (1996). A Feminist Mapping of Foucauldian Politics. In Susan J. Hekman (ed.), *Feminist Interpretations of Michel Foucault*. University Park: Pennsylvania State University Press, 241–264.

Lorde, A. (1983). An Open Letter to Mary Daly. In C. Moraga and G. Anzaldúa (eds), *This Bridge Called My Back: Writings by Radical Women of Color*. New York: Kitchen Table, Women of Color Press, 94–97.

Lorde, A. (1984). *Sister Outsider: Essays and Speeches*. Trumansburg, NY: The Crossing Press.

Luepnitz, D. (1992). Nothing in Common but Their First Names: The Case of Foucault and White. *Journal of Family Therapy* (Vol. 14 No. 3) 281–284.

Lugones, M. (1990). Playfulness, "World"-Travelling, and Loving Perception. In G. Anzaldúa (ed.), *Making Face, Making Soul = Haciendo Caras: Creative and Critical Perspectives by Feminists of Color*. San Francisco: Aunt Lute Foundation Books, 390–402.

Lugones, M. (1991). On the Logic of Pluralist Feminism. In C. Card (ed.), *Feminist Ethics*. Lawrence: University Press of Kansas, 35–44.

Lugones, M. and Spelman, E. (1990). Have We Got a Theory for You! Feminist Theory, Cultural Imperialism and the Demand for "The Woman's Voice". In A.Y Al-Hibri and M.A. Simons (eds), *Hypatia Reborn: Essays in Feminist Philosophy*. Bloomington: Indiana University Press, 18–33.

MacKinnon, C. (1989). *Toward a Feminist Theory of the State*. Cambridge, MA: Harvard University Press.

MacKinnon, L. (1993). Systems in Settings: The Therapist as Power Broker. *Australian and New Zealand Journal of Family Therapy* (Vol. 14 No. 3) 117–122.

McLean, C. (1996). The Politics of Men's Pain. In C. McLean, M. Carey and C. White (eds), *Men's Ways of Being*. Boulder, CO: Westview Press, 11–28.

McNay, L. (1992). *Foucault and Feminism: Power, Gender and the Self*. Cambridge: Polity Press.

McNay, L. (1994). *Foucault: A Critical Introduction*. Cambridge: Polity Press.

McPhie, L. and Chaffey, C. (1998). The Journey of a Lifetime: Group Work with Young Women who have Experienced Sexual Assault. *Gecko: A Journal of Deconstruction and Narrative Ideas in Therapeutic Practice* (Vol. 1) 3–34.

Madigan, S. (1992). The Application of Michel Foucault's Philosophy in the Problem Externalizing Discourse of Michael White. *Journal of Family Therapy* (Vol. 14 No. 3) 265–279.

Madigan, S. (1998). Destabilising Chronic Identities of Depression and Retirement: Inscription, Description, and Deciphering. In S. Madigan and I. Law (eds), *Praxis: Situating Discourse, Feminism and Politics in Narrative Therapies*. Vancouver, Canada: The Cardigan Press, 207–224.

Madigan, S. (2003). Counterviewing Injurious Speech Acts: Destabilizing Eight

Conversational Habits of Highly Effective Problems. *The International Journal of Narrative Therapy and Community Work* (No. 1) 43–59.

Mann, S. and Russell, S. (2002). Narrative Ways of Working with Women Survivors of Childhood Sexual Abuse. *The International Journal of Narrative Therapy and Community Work* (No. 3) 3–21.

Martin, B. (1988). Feminism, Criticism, and Foucault. In I. Diamond and L. Quinby (eds), *Feminism and Foucault: Reflections on Resistance*. Boston: Northeastern University Press, 3–19.

Martin, R. (1988). Truth, Power, Self: An Interview with Michel Foucault, October 25, 1982. In L. Martin, H. Gutman and P. Hutton (eds), *Technologies of the Self: A Seminar with Michel Foucault*. Amherst: University of Massachusetts Press, 9–15.

Mia (1998). Resilience is a Beautiful Word: Some Thoughtful Considerations in Relation to Working on Issues of Violence and Abuse. *Dulwich Centre Journal* (No. 4) 18–20.

Miller, J. (1994). *The Passion of Michel Foucault*. London: Flamingo.

Morris, M. (1988). The Pirate's Fiancée: Feminists and Philosophers, Or Maybe Tonight It'll Happen. In I. Diamond and L. Quinby (eds), *Feminism and Foucault: Reflections on Resistance*. Boston: Northeastern University Press, 21–42.

Myerhoff, B. (1986). Life Not Death in Venice: Its Second Life. In V. Turner and E. Bruner (eds), *The Anthropology of Experience*. Champaign: University of Illinois Press, 261–286.

Nehamas, A. (30 May 1988). Review of The Philosophical Discourse of Modernity by Jürgen Habermas. *The New Republic* (Vol. 198 Issue 3,828 No. 22) 32–36.

Noddings, N. (1984). *Caring: A Feminine Approach to Ethics and Moral Education*. Berkeley: University of California Press.

O'Farrell, C. (1989). *Foucault: Historian or Philosopher?* London: Macmillan.

O'Leary, P. (1998). Liberation from Self-Blame: Working with Men who have Experienced Childhood Sexual Abuse. *Dulwich Centre Journal* (No. 4) 24–40.

Orbach, S. and Eichenbaum, L. (1993). Feminine Subjectivity, Countertransference and the Mother–Daughter Relationship. In J. van Mens-Verhulst, K. Schreurs and L. Woertman (eds), *Daughtering and Mothering: Female Subjectivity Reanalysed*. London & New York: Routledge, 70–82.

O'Shane, P. (1993). Assimilation or Acculturation: Problems of Aboriginal Families. *Australian and New Zealand Journal of Family Therapy* (Vol. 14 No. 4) 196–198.

Owen, D. (November 1995). Genealogy as Exemplary Critique: Reflections on Foucault and the Imagination of the Political. *Economy and Society*. (Vol. 24 No. 4) 489–506.

Parker, I. (1997). Discursive Psychology. In D. Fox and I. Prilleltensky (eds), *Critical Psychology: An Introduction*. London: Sage, 284–298.

Parker, I. (1999a). Critical Psychology: Critical Links. *Annual Review of Critical Psychology* (Vol. 1) 3–18.

Parker, I. (ed.) (1999b). *Deconstructing Psychotherapy*. London: Sage.

Parker, I. and Shotter, J. (eds) (1990). *Deconstructing Social Psychology*. London: Routledge.

Parker, S., Nichter, M., Nichter, M., Vuckovic, N., Sims, C. and Ritenbaugh, C.

(Summer 1995). Body Image and Weight Concerns among African-American and White Adolescent Females: Differences that Make a Difference. *Human Organisation: Journal of the Society for Applied Anthropology* (Vol. 54 No. 2) 103–114.

Rabinow, P. (ed.) (1984). *The Foucault Reader*. London: Penguin.

Ransom, J. (1997). *Foucault's Discipline: The Politics of Subjectivity*. Durham & London: Duke University Press.

Raymond, J. (1986). *A Passion for Friends: Toward a Philosophy of Female Affection*. London: The Women's Press.

Reclaiming Our Stories, Reclaiming Our Lives: An Initiative of the Aboriginal Health Council of South Australia (1995). *Dulwich Centre Newsletter* (No. 1) 1–40.

Redekop, F. (1995). The "Problem" of Michael White and Michel Foucault. *Journal of Marital and Family Therapy* (Vol. 21 No. 3) 309–318.

Russell, S. and Carey, M. (2003). Feminism, Therapy and Narrative Ideas: Exploring Some Not So Commonly Asked Questions. *International Journal of Narrative Therapy and Community Work* (No. 2) 67–91.

Sawicki, J. (Fall 1986). Foucault and Feminism: Toward a Politics of Difference. *Hypatia: A Journal of Feminist Philosophy* (Vol. 1 No. 2) 23–36.

Sawicki, J. (1988). Identity Politics and Sexual Freedom: Foucault and Feminism. In I. Diamond and L. Quinby (eds), *Feminism and Foucault: Reflections on Resistance*. Boston: Northeastern University Press, 177–191.

Sawicki, J. (1991). *Disciplining Foucault: Feminism, Power, and the Body*. New York: Routledge.

Sawicki, J. (1998). Feminism, Foucault and "Subjects" of Power and Freedom. In J. Moss (ed.), *The Later Foucault: Politics and Philosophy*. London: Sage Publications, 93–107.

Seigfried, C.H. (1989). Pragmatism, Feminism, and Sensitivity to Context. In M.M. Brabeck (ed.), *Who Cares? Theory, Research, and Educational Implications of the Ethic of Care*. New York: Praeger, 63–83.

Seu, I. and Heenan, M. (eds) (1998). *Feminism and Psychotherapy: Reflections on Contemporary Theories and Practices*. London: Sage.

Silent Too Long (2–3 April 1998a). The Consequences of Community Silencing. Paper presented at *Kids First – Agenda for Change Conference*, Melbourne, Australia.

Silent Too Long (1998b). Your Voices Inspire Mine: Some Thoughtful Considerations in Relation to Working on Issues of Violence and Abuse. *Dulwich Centre Journal* (No. 4) 2–8.

Smart, B. (1998). Foucault, Levinas and the Subject of Responsibility. In J. Moss (ed.), *The Later Foucault: Politics and Philosophy*. London: Sage Publications, 78–92.

Smith, B. (1982). Racism and Women's Studies. In G.T. Hull, P.B. Scott and B. Smith (eds), *All the Women are White, All the Blacks are Men, But Some of Us are Brave: Black Women's Studies*. Old Westbury, NY: The Feminist Press, 48–51.

Spelman, E. (1991). The Virtue of Feeling and the Feeling of Virtue. In C. Card (ed.), *Feminist Ethics*. Lawrence: University Press of Kansas, 213–232.

Stacey, K. (1997). Alternative Metaphors for Externalizing Conversations. *Gecko:*

A Journal of Deconstruction and Narrative Ideas in Therapeutic Practice (Vol. 1) 29–51.

Strickling, B.L. (1988). Self-Abnegation. In L. Code, S. Mullett and C. Overall (eds), *Feminist Perspectives: Philosophical Essays on Method and Morals*. Toronto: University of Toronto Press, 190–201.

Swan, V. (1999). Narrative, Foucault and Feminism: Implications for Therapeutic Practice. In I. Parker (ed.), *Deconstructing Psychotherapy*. London: Sage, 103–114.

Tamasese, K. and Waldegrave, C. (1993). Cultural and Gender Accountability in the "Just Therapy" Approach. *Journal of Feminist Family Therapy* (Vol. 5 No. 2) 29–45.

Tannen, D. (1991). *You Just Don't Understand: Women and Men in Conversation*. London: Virago Press.

Taylor, C. (May 1984). Foucault on Freedom and Truth. *Political Theory* (Vol. 12 No. 2) 152–183.

Tomm, K. (1993). The Courage to Protest: A Commentary on Michael White's Work. In S. Gilligan and R. Price (eds), *Therapeutic Conversations*. New York: W.W. Norton, 62–80.

Tronto, J. (1987). Beyond Gender Difference to a Theory of Care. *Signs: Journal of Women in Culture and Society* (Vol. 12 No. 4) 644–663.

Tully, J. (1998). To Think and Act Differently: Foucault's Four Reciprocal Objections to Habermas' Theory. In S. Ashenden and D. Owen (eds), *Foucault Contra Habermas: Recasting the Dialogue between Genealogy and Critical Theory*. Thousand Oaks, CA: Sage Publications, 90–142.

Vintges, K. (2004). Endorsing Practices of Freedom: Feminism in a Global Perspective. In D. Taylor and K. Vintges (eds), *Feminism and the Final Foucault*. Urbana & Chicago: University of Illinois Press.

Waldegrave, C. (1990). Just Therapy: Social Justice and Family Therapy. *Dulwich Centre Newsletter* (No. 1) 5–46.

Waldegrave, C. (1998). The Challenges of Culture to Psychology and Postmodern Thinking. In M. McGoldrick (ed.), *Re-visioning Family Therapy: Race, Culture, and Gender in Clinical Practice*. New York: The Guilford Press, 404–413.

Waldegrave, C. and Tamasese, K. (1993). Some Central Ideas in the "Just Therapy" Approach. *Australian and New Zealand Journal of Family Therapy* (Vol. 14 No. 1) 1–8.

Ward, E. (1984). *Father–Daughter Rape*. London: The Women's Press.

We Appear Silent to People Who Are Deaf to What We Say (1989). *The Issue is ISM: Women of Color Speak Out*. Toronto, Canada: Sister Vision Press, 9–29.

Weingarten, K. (Spring 1998). The Small and the Ordinary: The Daily Practice of a Postmodern Narrative Therapy. *Family Process* (Vol. 37 No. 1) 3–15.

White, M. (Summer 1988/9). The Externalizing of the Problem and the Re-authoring of Lives and Relationships. *Dulwich Centre Newsletter*, 3–21.

White, M. (1991). Deconstruction and Therapy. *Dulwich Centre Newsletter* (No. 3) 21–40.

White, M. (28 February 1994a). *The Politics of Therapy: Putting to Rest the Illusion of Neutrality*. South Australia: Dulwich Centre Publications, 1–4.

White, M. (1994b). *Values*. South Australia: Dulwich Centre Publications, 1–5.

White, M. (1995). *Re-authoring Lives: Interviews and Essays*. South Australia: Dulwich Centre Publications.

White, M. (1997). *Narratives of Therapists' Lives*. South Australia: Dulwich Centre Publications.

White, M. (1999). Reflecting-Team Work as Definitional Ceremony Revisited. *Gecko: A Journal of Deconstruction and Narrative Ideas in Therapeutic Practice* (Vol. 2) 55–82.

White, M. (2000). *Reflections on Narrative Practice: Essays and Interviews*. South Australia: Dulwich Centre Publications.

White, M. (2001). The Narrative Metaphor in Family Therapy: An Interview. In D. Denborough (ed.), *Family Therapy: Exploring the Field's Past, Present and Possible Futures*. Adelaide, South Australia: Dulwich Centre Publications, 131–138.

White, M. (2002). Addressing Personal Failure. *The International Journal of Narrative Therapy and Community Work* (No. 3) 33–76.

White, M. and Epston, D. (1990). *Narrative Means to Therapeutic Ends*. New York: W.W. Norton & Co.

Wolf, N. (1992). *The Beauty Myth: How Images of Beauty are Used Against Women*. New York: Doubleday (Anchor Books).

Wylie, M.S. (November/December 1994). Panning for Gold. *The Family Therapy Networker*, 40–49.

INDEX

Where possible, entries avoid the use of self, e.g. **self acceptance** appears under **acceptance**. The term **self-policing** is used but most entries for this concept appear as subheadings of more specific terms.

discipline/disciplinary: practices, societal 13; power 16–17, 19; self 6
Discipline and Punish (Foucault) 14, 17, 19
disempowerment *see* empowerment/ disempowerment
dislike, self 2; *see also* blame; criticism; failure
domestic violence: attributing blame/ responsibility 32, 38–9; and ethics 89; and power relations 112–13; and self-policing 32, 38–9, 41, 122; therapy for 112–13, 125; *see also* rape; sexual abuse
domination: /exploitation 30, 87–9, 98; self 82, 85; *see also* ethics
doubt, self 25, 32, 33, 39
dualism 10, 12, 82, 93–4, 96; *see also* polarization

eating disorders 33, 43, 76, 90; narrative therapy for 51, 52, 125
educational system: narrative therapy 62; and self-policing 33, 34–5, 40, 122, 126
either/or thinking *see* polarization; *see also* dualism
emancipatory projects 110–11, 119, 120
emotional knowledge 96; *see also* feelings
empowerment/disempowerment 33, 34, 38, 39, 45, 66
enjoyment of self 83, 84
enlightenment 20; *see also* rational/ rationalism
entitlement sense 40, 113
epistemological relativism 57–8, 60
equality, ambiguity 34–5; *see also* ethics
essentialism (innate identity): Foucauldian discourse 8, 13–15, 20, 23, 24; general references 3, 9, 11; limitations 63; and mothering role 30; and narrative therapy 100, 102, 107–8, 110, 120; and power relations 15; rejection of concept 42, 54, 56, 58, 61; and unconscious mind 125; *see also* identity
ethics 78; of care *see* care (ethics of); Greek/classical 83–4, 85, 88, 97;

morality theory 89; narrative therapy 46, 57–60
ethnicity/ethnocentrism *see* difference; racism; white culture; white supremacy
exclusion 20; *see also* difference
expectations 33, 115; *see also* norms, societal
expert/s: language 56, 106, 107; mystique 66; surveillance 17; therapist discourse 9, 42, 45–7, 56, 60, 124; *see also* universal knowledge; specific intellectual model
exploitation/domination 30, 87–9, 98; *see also* care (ethics of)
expression, self 38
externalizing/internalizing narrative 9, 42, 49–51, 60, 123; *see also* individualizing/personal responsibility discourse; relational externalizing

failure, sense of 32–3, 82, 94, 98; and self-help 64; *see also* blame; criticism; dislike; judgement; shame
family restructuring 80, 114
family therapy 11; critiques 100, 105, 111–17, 121; social context of identity 111; *see also* narrative therapy
feelings: backlash 78; guilt 1, 2, 28, 31, 90; /hearing 67–8; negative 93; selfishness 90; shame/inadequacy 1, 2, 28, 32–3, 35, 95
female: development 72–3; identity 1, 27; as second sex 1, 9; *see also* mother/daughter relationships; parenting; self-policing
feminism 8, 11; consciousness-raising 98, 129; and disempowerment 66; and narrative therapy 66, 119, 121, 124; object-relations therapy 72, 125; perspective 27, 37, 124–5; solidarity 55, 119
femininity, norms 95–6
Fish, Vincent 111, 112, 114, 117
Foucault, Michel 4, 8, 9, 10, 11, 13, 20–5; *The Birth of the Clinic* 20; critiques 70; *Discipline and Punish* 14–19; *The History of Sexuality* 17, 94, 101; *Madness and Civilization* 20; *see also* discourses on specific

Date Due